TELL ME MORE

A COOKBOOK SPICED WITH
CAJUN TRADITIONS & FOOD MEMORIES

PUBLISHED BY

THE JUNIOR LEAGUE OF LAFAYETTE, INC.

LAFAYETTE, LOUISIANA

Copies of **TELL ME MORE** may be obtained from:

THE JUNIOR LEAGUE OF LAFAYETTE
100 Felecie Drive
Lafayette, LA 70506
Phone: (318) 988-2739 or 800-757-3651

ISBN: 0-935032-25-8

LCCN: 93-060210

First printing   20,000 Copies   November, 1993
Second printing   30,000 Copies   April, 1994

Printed in the USA by

WIMMER
The Wimmer Companies, Inc.
Memphis • Dallas

TABLE OF CONTENTS

ACKNOWLEDGEMENTS

Food memories, family traditions and good cooking are the essential ingredients that the Junior League of Lafayette has combined to create *Tell Me More*. This cookbook focuses on the family, folklore and fabulous food to create one of the most unique community cookbooks available. *Tell Me More* follows the successful legacy of the first two cookbooks published by the Junior League of Lafayette, *Talk About Good!* and *Talk About Good II*. It is through the graciousness and generosity of the League members, their families and friends who have shared their personal stories and family recipes that we were able to compile this warm and touching collection. The creative talents of local writer and editor, Bob Hamm, were used to enable us to present our cherished anecdotes in this charming and entertaining manner.

On our cover is an original work by renowned Cajun artist, Floyd Sonnier, entitled "Maman's Passing Down." The drawing depicts the central theme of our book, a grandmother relating family traditions to her two curious granddaughters. Mr. Sonnier is a well-known Cajun artist, and this marks his first major drawing in full color. Also included is a sampling of his pen-and-ink drawings that have been widely acclaimed for their artistic merit, and, perhaps more importantly, they have become more and more widely recognized as an authentic and important record of what it has meant and still means to be a Cajun. Floyd Sonnier is a uniquely gifted artist who for nearly two decades has devoted himself to portraying the Cajun lifestyle that he knows and loves so well. For more information on Mr. Sonnier and his art, please contact him at (318) 237-7104 or write him at P.O. Box 397, Scott, LA 70583.

COOKBOOK COMMITTEE

Lisa Mann Breaux	Becky Major Berthelot
Jennifer Bankston Briggs	Cammie Wood Dale
Dee Ann Posseno Jewell	Juliet Thibeaux McKay
Cindy Brown Melancon	Laurie Martin Smith

INTRODUCTION

This book is designed to serve a dual purpose. First, it offers recipes that are exciting to anyone who enjoys new culinary adventures, and finds joy in bringing delicious surprises to the family table.

Along with this, we have added features which reflect a basic truth about the dining experience: we all have special memories associated with meal time. Certain foods, particular occasions like Christmas or Thanksgiving Dinner, a special way a dish is cooked or served...such simple things call up these special memories. So with the recipes, we have included some poignant recollections that may entertain and amuse you, and add a more personal dimension to the listing of ingredients, measurements and directions in our unique collection of recipes. We hope they stir your own special memories of meal times past, and that as you read them, your thoughts will be *"tell me more."*

In Southwest Louisiana, where this book was prepared, there is a strong Acadian French influence. You will find the unique culture and traditions of the Cajuns reflected in many of the stories and recipes. The Cajun touch seems to add a certain happy spirit to all endeavors, and the Cajun way of life is typified by strong family values.

This is appropriate, since our second goal in presenting this book is to provide you with a way to turn cooking into fun, quality time with your family and to pass along food traditions and lasting memories, as you prepare some very delicious meals.

THE STORY OF THE CAJUNS

"In other parts of the world, little girls are made of sugar and spice and everything nice, while little boys are made of snips and snails and puppy dog tails. Little Cajun children, on the other hand, are made of gumbo, boudin and sauce piquante, crawfish stew and oreilles de cochon."

This whimsical passage from an essay called "What is a Cajun" points up a truism about the Acadian people of South Louisiana: food is more than sustenance; it is a keystone of the Cajun lifestyle.

The history of the unique dishes served at the Cajun dinner table is a vital part of the overall history of the Cajuns. The culinary traditions were born in times when these unusual people battled hardships of epic proportion. Reflected in the traditions and the recipes is the indomitable spirit and remarkable coping ability of a people who lived through years of brutal persecution and overpowering misery.

While today, Cajun dishes (or an approximation thereof) are often prepared by renowned chefs in the ultra-modern kitchens of fine restaurants and served in an elegant ambiance by waiters in dinner jackets, their origin was in a far different environment. For the most part, the classic Cajun dishes were developed by people who were poor in material goods and had to feed large families, (a home with a dozen children was not unusual), with whatever the fertile but harsh land around them produced. They gathered what was available in their isolated world of dense forests, swamps, coastal marshes and undeveloped prairies, and with a culinary magic that is theirs alone, transformed these simple ingredients into gourmet delights.

Cajun food is appreciated even more when the diner understands the story of these remarkable people.

Once, there was a place called Acadie.

Located on the Bay of Fundy in what is now Nova Scotia, the area was colonized in 1604 by hardy French farmers and fishermen who found such beauty, peace and joy in the family-like companionship of their neighbors in this simple setting, that they chose to give it a name derived from the Greek legend of the nearly Utopian province of Arcadia. Hence, the French colony became Acadie, and its people, Acadians.

The Acadians were willing and eager workers, and their indefatigable industry brought forth a rich natural bounty from their new land. They lived in idyllic simplicity. There was little currency; goods and services were bartered. There was perfect harmony with each other and with their Indian neighbors. Their land was truly Acadie.

Then rule of the area passed from the French to the British, and eventually conflict arose between those countries. The British were wary of these French Acadians in their midst, especially when they refused to sign an oath of allegiance to the Crown, unless it contained provisions for them to continue in their Catholic religion and protected them from having to bear arms against the enemies of the British Empire, (which could have included not only their French countrymen, but also their friends, the Indians).

The British concern over the loyalty of the Acadians was augmented by a concern for the fact that, in a colony now the possession of the crown, the choicest land belonged to these people of French origin.

The British felt the property so hard-earned by the Acadians should rightfully be inhabited by loyal British subjects.

The entire story is long and filled with Machiavellian maneuvers on the part of those who governed for Great Britain and were motivated both by military concerns and by the attractiveness of the real estate owned by the Acadians. The essence is that, in 1755, the Acadians saw their villages put to the torch, and found themselves being herded aboard British ships to be dispersed throughout the colonies. Families were torn apart, many never to see each other again. The ships were designed for cargo, not people, and the conditions in the holds were unbearable. Death from disease was rampant. Reception of the Acadians was not enthusiastic when ships docked in colonial ports. Largely Catholic Maryland accepted those who arrived there and made a place for them. At other ports, they were not allowed to disembark, and many died in the cramped holds of the ships. At some ports, they were allowed ashore but were pressed into a form of slavery called indentured servitude.

Exiled from Acadie, separated from loved ones, mistreated and enslaved, the Acadians might well have been destroyed as a culture. But they endured and survived. Hearing of Louisiana with its own French heritage, thousands of exiles began a tortuous journey through the North American wilderness. When they reached New Orleans, they again faced disappointment and despair. The French Creole nobility wanted nothing to do with these French farmers and fishermen.

Ironically, it was the Spanish, then in control of Louisiana, who provided land grants in Southwest Louisiana for the Acadians. The long hard journey ended in the lush coastal wilderness, where they would live in isolation until reasonably modern times, clinging to their language and customs and carving—from the marshes and swamps—another Acadie. Here they reaped the bounty of the bayous, rivers and the prolific Gulf waters, the untamed marshes and the great Atchafalaya swamp.

And, in their new Acadie, there was the same family spirit among neighbors and that same zest for living—undaunted by one of the most brutal ordeals in the history of the American continent.

The name Acadian has been contracted to "Cajun," an appellation resented at one time by descendants of the Nova Scotian exiles. Now, it is used with affection and respect—and has a bouncy ring that seems in keeping with the laughing way of life of these unique people. If there is any regret over the virtual demise of the word Acadian, it is because "Cajun" does not speak of Virgil's idyllic Arcadia, or of beautiful Acadie on the Bay of Fundy.

CAJUNS AT PLAY

No Food? No Fun!

One of the greatest influences on the early Cajun culture in Louisiana was the isolation of the Nova Scotian exiles from the outside world. Once settled in their new homes, they stayed close to them. Over the years, descendants of the exiles of Acadie married descendants of other exiles. They had little contact with the *Americains*, the non-Cajuns whom they associated with British colonists who treated them shabbily during their time of wandering. They continued to speak French, but their French was frozen in time. New words developed for new things in other French-speaking areas, but the isolated Cajuns did not have contact with the new things of the world, so there were no new words for them.

Formal contact with the Roman Catholic Church was infrequent. There was no church for them to attend in those early days, and priests visited only occasionally, so many Cajuns adapted the basics of the Catholic religion to their own needs and circumstances.

There were no doctors or medical facilities, but there were *traiteurs*, or healers, who practiced a folk medicine that often combined Catholicism with a bit of Voodoo, learned by those Cajuns who had been shipped to the West Indies during the *Grand Derangement* but made their way from there to Louisiana.

Social life centered around the home. Neighbors came together to fashion their own entertainment. Then, as now, food was central to any gathering of friends or family. Some examples:

The Boucherie

Among Cajuns, anything can be a celebration—including the butchering of a hog. Called a *Boucherie*, the occasion still brings together aunts, uncles, cousins and neighbors, all of whom participate, and leave with some of the byproducts of the butchering. Sharing animated conversation and often some cold beer or wine, the participants produce from the freshly killed hog *des tripes*, which their North Louisiana neighbors call "chitterlings," *p'tit sale* or salt meat, *andouille* sausage, pork meat patties called *plaltines*, the perennial favorite, *boudin*, which consists of rice and pork dressing stuffed in an edible casing, hog's head cheese, marinated pork or *grillades* and smoked meat for seasoning which Cajuns call *tasso*. Also from the Boucherie comes *chaudin*, the stuffed stomach of the hog, and *gratons*, the original Cajun snack food. Called "cracklins" in other parts of the country, *gratons* are produced along with a lard, another important byproduct of the Boucherie. The skin is scraped and the fat layer next to it rendered into lard for cooking, after which the skin and attached fat residue are fried into crisp, tasty *gratons*. They can be stored for months in buckets or jars, for occasional munching or inclusion in corn bread.

Courir du Mardi Gras

Mardi gras, or "Fat Tuesday," is celebrated in elaborate style in cities like New Orleans and Lafayette, as Catholics have one last fling before the beginning of the Lenten Season. In rural areas, the celebration bears little resemblance to the grand balls and giant parades of the cities. Country Cajuns celebrate *Courir du Mardi Gras*, or "run Mardi Gras." A masked crew on horseback, accompanied by a wagon or flat bed truck carrying non-riders and the necessary supply of liquid spirits, charge through the countryside on a mission involving food. The crew thunders up to farm houses along the route and halts a short distance away while their un-masked captain approaches to ask if the residents will "receive the Mardi Gras." Their object is to acquire poultry or other ingredients for a giant gumbo which will be consumed at day's end. Tradition calls for the crew to dance and sing for the contribution of, say, a fat hen, which the residents are happy to exchange for the entertainment. But tradition also calls for the fat hen to be flung into the yard and chased by the Mardi Gras revelers. The capture often ends up looking like a mud-wrestling contest, but ingredients are finally garnered from each farm house, and the giant gumbo feeds hundreds at the end of the zany ride.

The Cochon-de-Lait

Cochon-de-Lait translates as "milk pig." The tradition involves the roasting of a suckling pig over an open fire. Often throughout an entire night, men folk of the neighborhood keep watch over the roasting pig, turning it on a wire contraption over the open flames. In Avoyelles Parish, which claims the culinary tradition as its own, the hours of watching and turning the pig are times of great camaraderie, moderate imbibing and telling of tall tales.

The Cajun Straight Race

With the coming of professional racing and pari-mutuel betting to Cajun Country, the colorful tradition of straight racing has almost died away. It began informally at those long-ago gatherings of friends and family when young men would ride over on horses or mules, most of which had been working to the plow only hours earlier. An enthusiasm for racing developed, (to the point that pastors were some times exasperated when the men sent their wives and children inside to mass, while they raced their horses around the churchyard), and over the years, the races became somewhat formalized, with the establishment of tracks that were usually two straight lanes separated by a rail fence. The separation was necessary because horse-owners found their animals could move faster with young, light-weight boys on their backs. The railing was protection from being trampled if one of the little jockeys should fall from his mount. There was no betting window, and no rules existed for racing. All bets were side bets between owners or spectators. A mule could run against a Shetland pony. If the bet was with daylight, there had to be daylight showing between the rump of the leader and the nose of the other horse, or the leader didn't win. Sometimes two track-wise old horses would run without riders. Owners would tie a couple of rock-filled beer cans to their saddle horns and the rattling would spur them on.

The food connection? The little commercial tracks that eventually sprang up usually featured a lean-to building that was a concession stand of sorts, and adjoining it was a big barbecue pit. The menu consisted of cold beer or soft drinks, and a sandwich made by tossing a piece of barbecued pork, bone and all, on a piece of bread and swabbing it with a thick, rich, peppery Cajun sauce.

The Crawfish Boil

A *crayfish* is a little mud bug that is found in ditches in some parts of the country, and ordinarily used for bait. A *Crawfish* is a sought-after crustacean of the Cajun Country which is prepared in a myriad of ways—all incredibly delicious. It can be the central ingredient of a gumbo, bisque, etouffee, stew or even a pie. But for big, happy outdoor gatherings among the Cajuns, the preferred style of preparation is simply boiling them, then peeling them, maybe dipping them in a tangy sauce and devouring them. The choice meat is in the tail, and any Cajun can show you the almost instant way to peel it. Real crawfish aficionados go further, sucking the rich fat—saturated with seasoning from the boiling pot—from what is commonly referred to as the head of the crawfish, even though it constitutes most of the body, other than tail and pincers. The crawfish boil, although its origins do not go back as far as other Cajun activities, is probably the most popular of all the traditional Cajun social gatherings.

These are occasions peculiar to the Cajuns. Events that are not historically their very own center around food, also. Food is brought to the new mother when a baby is born. After that child's christening, there is a veritable feast, with perhaps an even larger one after his confirmation. On a birthday or any holiday, tables are piled high with an immense variety of meats, vegetables and desserts. And not one dessert, mind you. A dozen different ones would be considered proper. At his wedding, the tables bulge and sag under the weight of the variety of delicious concoctions. And, when a friend is claimed by death, neighbors arrive with food for the distraught family—a tangible gesture of kindness and concern.

Food is part of the Cajun heritage, culture and lifestyle. Eating is a special occasion, even when just sitting down with the immediate family. It has been said that Cajuns don't eat to live—they live to eat. In today's health-conscious world, this may be changing—but as long as Cajuns gather, there will be fun...and there will be food.

INFLUENCES ON CAJUN COOKING

The lifestyle of the early Cajuns in Louisiana greatly influenced the meals they prepared and the way they prepared them. In the beginning, there was virtually no money to be had, and in their profound isolation, there would have been no grocery stores in which to make purchases, had funds been available. They had to make do with what was available in their limited world.

Wild game and seafood were plentiful. Most Cajuns were able to acquire farm animals, and while cows were valuable for their milk and not often slaughtered, hogs offered an immense variety of culinary opportunities. Pork, poultry, seafood and wild game were the primary foodstuffs. The way in which they were prepared was influenced by a number of cultures.

There remained the culinary traditions of their original homeland, although their part of France was not, like Paris, noted for its *haute cuisine*. In Acadie, as in Louisiana, there was much contact with the Indians, and this influence can be found in their cooking. Some of the exiles settled in the West Indies before reaching Louisiana and were influenced by culinary traditions there. Also, there was contact with the Spanish who ruled Louisiana during the early days of the Cajun migration, so there is a taste of Old Spain in some Cajun dishes. Contrary to the Hollywood stereotype, all Cajuns did not long remain poor but happy swamp dwellers. Many prospered in farming, and records show that there was a significant percentage of the Cajun population that owned slaves. Thus, Cajun cooking also shows the influence of the African-American culture.

It needs to be noted that, in semi-tropical Louisiana, growing of rich spices is common. Peppers are so plentiful as to provide the basis of a major industry—making of world-famed Tabasco sauce. The availability of spices and the influence of several cultures devoted to their use in cooking, contributed to their popularity with the Cajuns.

So Cajun cooking may be deemed the result of necessity, environment, influence of other cultures—and a little magic.

LAISSEZ LES BON TEMPS ROULER

Whether it was on the back porch, under a giant oak or china-ball tree, or on dance floors, Cajuns always enjoyed music and dancing. They would unashamedly "let the good times roll".

Floyd Sonnier

CAJUN APPETIZERS

If appetizers were, in truth, intended to whet one's appetite for the meal to come, they probably would never have been prepared in my mother's house. Everyone's appetite was whetted—to razor sharpness—the minute they came within sniffing distance of my mother's kitchen. Rather than a stimulus for the appetite, Mom's appetizers usually offered a sampling of some of the dishes that were not part of the main course at the moment, but which, at another time and in larger quantities, would be elevated to that place of honor. Some (or all) of the following were served as appetizers, but guests didn't fill up on them, because they wanted to retain a healthy appetite for what they knew would be a super delicious main course.

- Soup was usually not an option. Instead, a cup (not a bowl; that could be the main course) of shrimp and okra gumbo was usually offered as an appetizer.

- In place of the cocktail sausage, she served bite-sized portions of Boudin —delicious rice and pork dressing in an edible casing.

- Her appetizer offering frequently included bite-sized catfish fillets, crisply fried in a seasoned batter.

- Another favorite was salty Louisiana oysters on the half shell, with a spicy, delicious sauce on the side.

- Very special guests might be treated to tiny Crawfish Pies. C'est magnifique!

- The cheese on her Cajun canapés was usually hog's head cheese.

- Gratons (cracklins) supplanted chips. (No dips with cracklins, please.)

Modern science had not given us soft-shell crawfish in Mom's day, but I'm sure that would have ranked as one of her favorite appetizers.

APPETIZERS, JELLIES, PICKLES AND SAUCES

BAKED BRIE

1 (6-8") round Brie cheese

Pie crust (homemade or store bought)

One of the following:
1) ¼ cup brown sugar, ¼ cup chopped pecans
2) Apricot preserves
3) Peppered jelly and minced garlic

Peel outer layer of cheese - roll out pie crust large enough to encase cheese. Place ½ of 1, 2, or 3 in center of crust, then Brie and remainder of topping and gently fold crust together, pinching edges. Close all openings. Carefully turn over. Bake at 350 degrees for 30 minutes.

Bonnie Broussard

CHEESE BALL

1 pound grated sharp cheddar cheese
1 cup finely chopped pecans
¾ cup mayonnaise

1 medium grated onion
1 clove pressed garlic
1 teaspoon Tabasco
1 cup chopped pecans

Combine cheddar cheese, 1 cup pecans, mayonnaise, onion, garlic and Tabasco. Shape into ball (which will harden once it is refrigerated.) Pat remaining pecans into ball. Refrigerate.

Terri Foret

CHEESE ROUND MOLD

1 pound grated sharp cheddar cheese
1 cup chopped pecans
¾ cup mayonnaise
1 finely chopped small to medium onion

1 finely chopped clove garlic
½ teaspoon Tabasco sauce
Strawberry preserves

Combine ingredients (except preserves) mixing with a spoon. Spray a round mold with no stick cooking spray. Put mixture into mold. Refrigerate two hours. Remove cheese round onto plate. Spoon preserves in center of cheese round. Serve with crackers. (To loosen dip from mold, heat bottom of mold dish slightly, then it should turn over easily onto serving dish.)

Pamela Smith

DONNA'S CHEESE-IN-THE-ROUND

2 packages (8 ounce)
softened cream cheese
1 can (8½ ounce) drained
crushed pineapple

¼ cup chopped green
pepper
1 tablespoon minced onion
1 tablespoon seasoning salt
2 cups chopped pecans

Mix together everything but pecans. Roll into two balls then roll in chopped pecans. Freezes well.

Anne Simon

SNAPPY CHEESE BALLS

1 jar English sharp cheese
1 jar jalapeño cheese
2 sticks butter
¼ teaspoon salt

¼ teaspoon dry mustard
Dash red pepper
2 cups + 4 tablespoons flour
Stuffed olives

Blend cheeses and butter together in mixer. Season with salt, red pepper, dry mustard. Add flour gradually. Cover stuffed olive with mixture and roll into ball. Place on greased cookie sheet and chill overnight. Bake at 375 degrees for 10 minutes. (These may be packed in freezer bags and frozen uncooked. When baking, increase temperature to 400 degrees for 12-15 minutes.)

Marianne Schneider

CHILI RELLENO DIP

2 large peeled and chopped
tomatoes
1 small can chopped green
chilies

1 small can chopped black
olives
4 chopped green olives
3 tablespoons oil
1½ teaspoons garlic salt

Mix well. Add salt and pepper to taste. Chill. Serve with Doritos.

Lisa Ann Baer

OREILLES DE COCHON

Newcomers to Acadiana find the names of Cajun food almost as intriguing as the dishes themselves. Some complain, however, that there is a mischievous deceptiveness in the Cajun names. For instance, what could be more appealing than a dish with the ear-pleasing title of "Frommage de Tête?" And how many visitors have experienced the delicious taste, then listened aghast as they were told that "Frommage de Tête" is Cajun for hog's head cheese?

On the other hand, many have turned up their noses at "Oreilles de Cochon," which translates "Pigs Ears," only to learn that it is an incredibly delicious pastry which got its name from its shape, rather than from any association with barnyard animals. Oreilles de Cochon—light, flaky and spread with rich cane syrup—is a rare and wonderful dessert treat.

HOG'S HEAD CHEESE

5 pounds pig feet or fresh hocks
5-6 pounds Boston roast, cut in chunks
2-3 chopped large onions
2 chopped bell peppers
2-3 cloves garlic
2 tablespoons vinegar
Salt, black pepper, crushed red pepper to taste
2 bunches finely chopped green onion
1 bunch finely chopped parsley

Put all ingredients except parsley and green onions in a large heavy pot. Cover with water until about one inch over meat. Bring to a boil, reduce heat to low simmer. Cook 3-4 hours. Strain out meat. Add green onions and parsley to liquid. Carefully remove all bone from feet and hocks. Chop meat but not too finely. Add back to liquid. Taste for seasoning. When hot it should taste a little over salty and peppery. Pour into any size pans or molds (best if it is 2 inches deep) and let cool. Refrigerate overnight. If after cooling you feel it needs more salt or pepper you can melt it and repour and cool again.

John Major

LUNCH AT LA LA'S

My favorite food memory is not of exotic dishes served in a plush environment on a momentous occasion. I (and many of my friends) have fond memories of something very simple: my mother's pimento cheese. When I was growing up, in a simple time, we lived a short distance from the school and always walked home for lunch. Friday, I brought an entourage with me. My friends knew that Friday was the day my mother fixed her wonderful pimento cheese—the likes of which they had never tasted—so they were my companions for lunch. What fun we had, and what a treat was "La La's Pimento Cheese." When I run into the old gang now, we reminisce about those Friday lunches. Every Friday, I pay loving tribute to my mother as I fix pimento cheese for my family.

PIMENTO CHEESE SPREAD

1 jar (4 ounce) diced pimento
2 hard boiled eggs, chopped
2 cups shredded American cheese
3 tablespoons mayonnaise
Dash of red pepper (optional)

Mix all together. Spread on crackers or use for sandwiches. Delicious!

Now, every Friday morning, I make pimento cheese for my family and I remember my mother.

Barbara Guidry Bills

GUACAMOLE APPETIZER FOR SIX

3 halves avocado
1 tablespoon chopped cilantro
1 teaspoon finely chopped jalapeño pepper
1 tablespoon finely chopped red onion

1-2 tablespoons medium hot salsa
1 teaspoon salt
½ teaspoon oregano
¼ teaspoon garlic powder
¼ teaspoon white pepper
¼ freshly squeezed lime
1 small diced tomato

Mix everything together with two forks. Toss a few diced tomato pieces on top for garnish. Serve with corn chips.

Shirley Leonpacher

SEVEN LAYER DIP

1 can bean dip
6 ounces of guacamole dip
8 ounces of sour cream
1 envelope taco seasoning mix
½ very finely chopped purple onion

2-3 finely chopped tomatoes (very ripe)
8 ounces grated sharp cheddar cheese
1 small can sliced black olives

In approximately a 12 inch round deep dish (sides about 1 inch), layer the above ingredients. Spread bean dip; spread guacamole on top. Mix taco seasoning mix with sour cream in bowl; add this on top of guacamole. Spread chopped onion on top next. Spread chopped tomatoes on top next. Spread grated cheese next. Place sliced olives last on top. Serve along side large bag of plain tostada chips.

Pam Smith

BLACK-EYED PEA DIP

2 cans drained black-eyed peas
1 stick margarine
1 roll jalapeño cheese
1 roll garlic cheese

1 medium chopped onion
4 pods minced garlic
2 tablespoons chopped jalapeño

Combine ingredients, microwave until melted. Serve with corn chips.

Amy Ellender

Garbanzo Bean Dip

1 tablespoon olive oil or 2 strips of bacon
3-5 minced garlic cloves
1 link of sausage (optional)
1 (16 ounce) can garbanzo beans
½ can of 8 ounce tomato sauce
1 teaspoon of cumin powder
1 teaspoon salt
1 teaspoon pepper

Heat oil or bacon and sauté garlic in skillet (add sausage at this time.) Add beans and cook on medium heat until tender, about 15 minutes. Add half can of tomato sauce and spices. Mash some of the beans to form a paste consistency. May be served as dip with chips or over white rice.

Grace Carrell

Black Bean Tostadas

3-4 cloves of garlic
2 sprigs of fresh rosemary pulled off stem (discard stem) or 2 teaspoons dried (if fresh is unavailable)
1 (16 ounce) can black beans, drained
1 package (1 dozen) tostadas
8 ounces goat cheese
1 bunch chopped cilantro (cut off stems and discard)

Put garlic and rosemary in food processor. Chop finely. Add drained black beans to food processor and blend together. Spread tostadas evenly with black bean mixture. Slice goat cheese into 12 even pieces and crumble over black bean mix. Put tostadas in preheated 350 degree oven for 10-15 minutes until goat cheese is soft (not melted). Remove from oven. Top with chopped cilantro and serve warm. Can be folded and eaten like a taco!

Kellee Cheatham

Ham Roll-Ups

1 package ham
1 small package cream cheese
1 jar olives

Lay ham flat in single layer. Spread cream cheese over layer of ham. Add olives. Roll lengthwise in jelly rolls and freeze. When ready, cut into bite size pieces.

Laurie Smith
Cindy Melancon

ANNETTE'S HOT & SPICY PARTY MIX

2 sticks oleo
Salt
Red pepper
Black pepper
Garlic powder
15 drops Tabasco
¼ cup Worcestershire sauce

3 tablespoons hot garlic sauce
1 cup whole pecan halves
½ box rice cereal
½ box corn cereal
½ box wheat cereal
1 cup mixed nuts

Preheat oven to 300 degrees. In a large aluminum roasting pan melt 1½ sticks oleo (place in preheated oven to melt oleo). Then add generous amounts of salt, red and black pepper, garlic powder to melted oleo. Also add Tabasco (10-15 drops) sauce, Worcestershire sauce, and garlic sauce. Mix well. Then add nuts -mix well. Add ½ box of each of the cereals. Slice remaining ½ stick of oleo into parts and distribute over cereal mixture. Bake at 300 degrees for 45 minutes. Every 15 minutes, remove from oven and mix well. Adjust seasonings if needed. Could be stored for later use and can be frozen also.

Annette Bradley

CAJUN STUFFED MUSHROOMS

½ pound bulk Cajun pork sausage
1 cup chopped onions
¼ cup chopped bell pepper
½ teaspoon salt
½ teaspoon garlic powder
½ teaspoon cayenne pepper

1 cup water
¾ cup quick rice
¼ cup chopped parsley
24 large stuffing mushrooms, cut stems and save
2 cups mayonnaise
1½ cups Parmesan cheese

Brown sausage, onions, bell pepper and mushroom stems. Add salt, garlic powder and cayenne pepper. Add water and bring to a boil. Add quick rice and parsley. Cover and remove from heat. Let stand for 15 minutes. Meanwhile, blend mayonnaise and cheese. Combine half of mayonnaise mixture to all of cooked sausage-rice. Stuff mushrooms with this and spoon remaining mayonnaise-cheese mixture on top of mushrooms. Place in 9 x 12 baking dish and bake at 350 degrees for 35 minutes. Mushrooms will appear puffy and golden when done.

Sky Salter

Acadiana Culinary Classic 1992 Le Petit Classique second place winner.

MAKE-YOUR-OWN STEAK APPETIZERS

3 pounds top round steak - about 2 inches thick
2 teaspoons vegetable oil

Assorted fruits and vegetables:
  water chestnuts
  pineapple chunks
  baby corn
  pickled mushrooms
  celery sticks
  scallion pieces
  red bell pepper strips
  green bell pepper strips
Small jar honey mustard

Heat oven to 450 degrees. Brush top of top round steak with oil. Place on lightly oiled rack in roasting pan. Roast 30 minutes, or until cooked to desired degree of doneness. Let stand 20 minutes before carving. Slice steak across grain into very thin strips, about 5 inches long by 1½ inches wide. Cut each strip in half. Arrange steak on large carving board or platter with an assortment of fruits and vegetables such as those listed above. Let guests make their own appetizers by rolling up one or more fruits or vegetables in steak strip. Secure rolls with wooden toothpicks. Serve with honey mustard sauce for dipping or spooning over steak rolls.

48-50 appetizers

Lise Anne Dumond Slatten

PIZZA APPETIZERS

1 pound hot pork sausage
1 pound ground meat
2 tablespoons oregano
½ teaspoon garlic salt

½ teaspoon Worcestershire
1 pound grated Velveeta cheese
1 loaf Party Rye bread

Brown sausage and ground meat. Drain off fat. Add remaining ingredients and mix well until cheese melts. Spread on slices of rye bread. Freeze on cookie sheet. Then bag in plastic bags and keep in freezer until ready to serve. Bake at 400 degrees for 10 minutes.

Lisa Ann Baer

SPINACH PINWHEELS

1 (10 ounce) package frozen chopped spinach (thawed and drained
1 (8 ounce) package of softened cream cheese
½ cup (2 ounces) grated Parmesan cheese
1 (2 ounce) jar chopped pimento, drained
⅛ teaspoon ground nutmeg
1 (8 ounce) can crescent rolls

Combine spinach, cheeses, pimento and nutmeg. Mix well until blended. Unroll crescent roll dough and form into four rectangles and press seams together. Spread each rectangle with spinach mixture. Roll each rectangle, starting at short end. Cut each roll into 8 slices. Place cut side down on ungreased cookie sheet. Bake at 375 degrees for 10-12 minutes.

32 appetizers

Dawn Amy

TORTILLA ROLL-UPS

2 large packages of softened cream cheese
4 cloves minced garlic
¼ cup chopped green onions
¼ cup chopped jalapeño peppers
10-12 flour tortillas

Combine cream cheese, garlic, green onions and jalapeños. Spread on tortillas. Roll-up jelly roll fashion. Place seam down and sliced in 1 inch pieces. Serve with salsa and/or guacamole!

Mimi Francez

OYSTER/SAUSAGE APPETIZER

2 pounds smoked sausage
2 cups white wine
1 teaspoon Tabasco sauce
½ teaspoon garlic powder
½ teaspoon salt
Juice of one lemon
1 quart oysters (drained)

Slice sausage into bite size pieces and cook in skillet in 1 cup of wine and all of the seasonings until most of the liquid is absorbed. Add ½ to 1 cup of remaining wine and the drained oysters. Simmer until oyster edges curl. Garnish with parsley and green onion and serve from chafing dish with toothpicks.

Serves 30

Martha Moreau Latiolais

SHRIMP GOUDA IN PUFF PASTRY

1 pound cooked chopped
  shrimp
½ cup chopped green onions
½ cup chopped fresh parsley
2 tablespoons butter
2 cloves minced garlic
1 tablespoon seafood
  seasoning
⅓ cup heavy cream
3 tablespoons Parmesan
  cheese
¼ cup dry Vermouth
½ package frozen puff pastry
1 pound round Gouda
  cheese, cut in large slices
Melted butter

Simmer butter, shrimp, onions, parsley, and garlic until tender. Add cream, Parmesan cheese, Vermouth, and seasoning. Simmer until liquid is consumed. Set aside to cool. Defrost ½ package of puff pastry to room temperature. Place one pastry on baking sheet. Add Gouda cheese in center. Add shrimp mixture on top of cheese. Fold pastry over cheese and shrimp. Seal edges. Brush with melted butter. Bake at 350 degrees for 30 minutes.

You may substitute crawfish in place of shrimp.

10 servings

Mimi Francez

APPETIZER ANTIPASTO SPREAD

1 (8 ounce) can mushrooms
1 (14 ounce) can artichoke
  hearts
1 (4 ounce) jar pitted green
  olives

1 (4½ ounce) can chopped
  black olives
1 bell pepper
2 celery stalks

Marinade:

⅓ cup olive oil
½ cup vegetable oil
¼ cup minced dry onion
1 teaspoon pepper
1 teaspoon onion powder

2 teaspoons Italian
  seasoning
1 teaspoon salt
¾ cup white vinegar
1 teaspoon garlic powder

Drain first 4 ingredients. Process all ingredients in food processor (until rice sized) one at a time and place in large bowl.

Marinade: Boil all marinade ingredients for 2 minutes. Pour over vegetables and chill. Serve with crisp pita bread wedges or your favorite crackers.

7 cups   **Tina Roy**

CAVIAR PIE

1 (16 ounce) package soft
  cream cheese
1 (12 ounce) carton sour
  cream

1 finely diced onion
3 grated hard boiled eggs
2 (4 ounce) jars black
  caviar, good quality

Use cream cheese to line bottom and sides of 9 inch glass pie plate. Add other ingredients in order listed above. Serve with melba toast or other crackers. Best to make ahead and put in refrigerator overnight. Add caviar right before serving. May use red caviar at holiday time.

Lise Anne Dumond Slatten

ROASTED GARLIC

3 whole cloves garlic
¼ cup olive oil

¼ teaspoon thyme
¼ teaspoon salt and pepper

Cut off top of garlic and sit on pan. Mix all ingredients and pour over garlic. Bake at 350 degrees for 15 minutes and 250 degrees for 60 minutes. Continue to baste while cooking. Spread over crackers or melba rounds.

Jennifer Briggs

FRIDAYS

In our Catholic family, we observed Friday as a day of abstinence, on which no meat was ever eaten. But the evening meal on Friday was one to which we looked forward, especially in the summer time. Mom always fixed a refreshing summer meal of scrambled eggs, tuna, corn on the cob, sliced fresh tomatoes, and sometimes catfish caught that day in the nearby river. Every meal was topped off with something sweet—but not a sugary dessert. We had something like delicious home-made fig preserves on fresh sliced bread with butter.

FIG PRESERVES

4 quarts of figs
4 quarts of sugar
1 ½ cups water

Cut stems off of figs and then wash figs quickly in cold water. Combine sugar and water in large pot. Bring to a boil. Add figs. Cook until desired thickness of juice. Seal in sterilized jars.

Marguerite LeBlanc

Catholics now eat meat on Friday, but while traditions may change, memories of those special summer evening meals will always remain.

HOT PEPPER JELLY (GREEN OR RED)

½ cup ground fresh hot
    peppers
7½ cups sugar
1 teaspoon salt

1½ cups white vinegar
1 small bottle liquid Certo
5 drops of red or green food
    coloring (if desired)

Boil peppers, sugar, vinegar, and salt 8-10 minutes (rolling boil). Add Certo and boil about 3 more minutes, add coloring. Pour in sterilized jelly jars.

May Louviere

MOM'S PEPPER JELLY

1¼ cups apple cider vinegar
¾ cup chopped bell pepper
¼ cup hot peppers

6½ cups sugar
1 bottle or package Certo
    pectin

Mix vinegar, peppers, and sugar and bring this to a rolling boil, approximately 2 minutes. Remove from fire, let stand 10 minutes. Add Certo and stir, let stand 10 minutes, then skim top, pour into warm jars.

Leslie Sandlin

REFRIGERATOR PICKLES

3 thinly sliced cucumbers
1 chopped bell pepper
1 chopped sweet onion
2 teaspoons celery seed

1 tablespoon salt
¾ cup sugar
½ cup white vinegar

Mix vegetables gently. Add remaining ingredients. Refrigerate, covered, at least 2 hours. Keeps up to three weeks.

Charlotte Sicard

SUNDAYS (AND OTHER SPECIAL GATHERINGS)

Virtually all my family memories center around food. Every gathering was for a barbecue or crawfish boil or a scrumptious feast at the dinner table. My most pleasant memories of my Dad are of his outdoor cooking—preparing giant crawfish boils six or seven times a summer with the customary 10 pounds per person; smoking giant roasts for as many as 600 people; cooking frog legs, shrimp or fresh fish on a raft in the river. Mom, a home economics graduate, did the indoor cooking, so it was always balanced and nutritious—and always delicious. I remember on Sundays that Dad listened to Mario Lanza at meal time, and that he taught us responsible use of alcoholic beverages by serving a glass of wine, well diluted with water, to the children.

We learned to cook by watching. There was a bench by the stove, and we sat and watched Mom bake her delicious pies, cakes and biscuits, and we always gathered around as Dad made a tub of his famous Barbecue Sauce. We watched and learned.

A special food memory is of Sunday nights, which was "do-it-yourself night" at our house. The kids were allowed to fix whatever they wanted to eat—supposedly to give Mom a rest. The fact was that

ALBIN'S BARBECUE SAUCE

4 onions
½ bunch celery
2 bell peppers
4 cloves garlic
1 cup vegetable oil
1 gallon ketchup or 4 (32 ounce) bottles
½ gallon water
4 lemons - juice only
4 tablespoons chili powder
Salt
Black pepper
½ small bottle Worcestershire sauce
½ ounce mustard
½ bottle liquid smoke
1 cup brown sugar

Chop onions, celery, bell pepper and garlic. In a 5 gallon pot, sauté these ingredients in oil until transparent. Add all remaining ingredients. Mix well. Bring to a boil. Reduce to a very low temperature and cook uncovered for approximately three hours stirring often.

3 to 3½ gallons of sauce

Gretchen Allen

she had to clean the kitchen after the onslaught, so there wasn't much rest. But it was wonderful for us. Some of us had home-made cinnamon rolls made from canned biscuits, others who were less industrious might just have cereal, and some ate soup right out of the can. Whatever we had, we finished it in time to watch Bonanza.

When I think of the family together, and the fun we had, I always think of the many ways that food was a part of our lives.

———————

CHUCH'S TARTAR SAUCE

3 cups mayonnaise
8 garlic pods
1 heaping teaspoon dry
   mustard

1 dill pickle (6" long)
1 small onion

Blend all ingredients in a blender.

Joan Blanchet

GREEN PICANTE SAUCE

2 medium to large tomatoes
1 medium onion
½ medium green pepper
2 or more jalapeños
15 or more green chilies

1 clove garlic
2 teaspoons chili pepper
½ teaspoon sugar
⅛ teaspoon salt (or to taste)
1 teaspoon vinegar

Boil tomatoes until soft (about 10 to 15 minutes of full boil). Blend in blender the onion, green pepper, jalapeño, green chilies, garlic, chili pepper, sugar, salt and vinegar. (The more chilies the hotter the sauce). Add the juicy hot tomatoes to the blender. Slowly blend making sure all is chopped and mixed together well.

Janet Perkins

THE HUNT

There is so much more to the hunt than that moment of truth when game is in your sights—and for a second in time you are joined with those generations to whom a successful hunt was essential to providing food for the family table.

THE #1 VENISON MARINADE

1 ½ cups oil
¾ cup soy sauce
½ cup Worcestershire sauce
2 tablespoons dry mustard
⅓ cup vinegar
1 tablespoon pepper
1 ¼ teaspoons salt
1 teaspoon parsley
⅓ cup lemon juice
1 teaspoon garlic powder

Add ingredients together in sequence, as listed, in large bowl. Stir well, pour over venison, and allow to marinade for 24 hours in refrigerator. This marinade may be used on venison that is to be barbecued or roasted in oven. If venison is barbecued, the venison may be basted with the marinade as it cooks on the pit.

Terry McFarland

I remember those Novembers of my boyhood when I would go with male relatives into the prolific wilderness of North Louisiana and East Texas and, there in the deep woods share an experience that is indelibly inscribed on my memory and on that of any other youngster who has known a similar adventure.

I remember the spirit of camaraderie, the conversations around the camp fire that William Faulkner has called "the best of all talk," and the rich aroma of food cooking over an open fire in the cool, clean November air.

When one of the hunters brought venison to the camp, his pride was matched by our anticipation. The bitter wild taste eradicated by the 24 hours in a special marinade, the delicious meat was cooked over an open fire, absorbing the rich smoke. I have pleasant memories of fine restaurants, with marvelous cuisine and ambiance, but no food memory is more precious than those from my boyhood, when we gathered around the campfire in that special world of the hunter, and feasted on campfire-cooked beans and smoked, cooked venison.

SUGAR CANE

South Louisiana—rich in sugar cane—has been called the "Sugar Bowl of America." In earlier times, the land of the Cajuns was dotted with small sugar mills, where operators of small farms brought their cane—at the season called "grinding"—to be transformed into sugar and cane syrup. At these mills, an experienced old mule would walk slowly and steadily in a circle, activating the machinery which turned the big rollers that ground the juice from the cane into big open kettles. The juice was progressively condensed by boiling and dipped from one kettle to another until in the final stage it was granulated. From the last operation, the cane syrup (seigne' des barques) was collected.

Like anything else in Cajun Country in the old days, "grinding" often became a social occasion, with young people gathering at the small mills to socialize while sampling the product in all its stages. There was cold juice fresh from the rollers, then hot juice from the kettles. Finally came the real treat, called "cuite"—a mixture of sugar and molasses from the last cooking, C'est bon, cher!

Not to be overlooked—now as then—is the raw cane, still in the stalk. When the big trucks roll at grinding season with the cane buggies in tow, little children (and some adults) still follow in their wake to pick up stalks that tumble out accidentally, and which they peel and chew with sweet, sweet satisfaction.

"SPRING CAJUN WEDDING"

Besides drawings of children, Cajun wedding scenes are the most popular and are always in great demand. Again I went to the old family album and found a couple in a wedding of the turn-of-the-century. The photograph was in a studio setting. I created a scene that portrays a young couple proudly posing in front of the home they'll start their life together in and the horse and buggy that he most-likely owns; which he's prepared to share with his bride. In all likelihood their new life would be with the hardships of farming. And I'm sure they were prepared for it.

Floyd Sonnier

FRENCH BREAD

The aroma of particular foods can be just as provocative of special memories as the taste—sometimes even more so. The smell of fresh bread is the memory thread that binds together for me those precious memories of Sunday morning, Six O'clock Mass, and Papa.

I remember the eight-block walk we made each Sunday to early Mass, while thoughts of religion mingled with anticipation of the delights that would follow when Papa led us across the street to Mr. Jack's Bakery. It was a family tradition. Even before we entered the shop, the sweet, yeasty smell of bread fresh from the oven greeted us. It seemed to come to us from the doorways, windows, transoms, even the rooftop. After the customary purchase of two loaves, Papa let my younger brother and me each carry a hot, crisp loaf home.

There, the bread was quickly unwrapped and broken or torn into eagerly awaited pieces for all of us. There was probably butter for the bread, but I don't remember it, and since it was before I knew about peanut butter, we probably ate it plain. I know that after we finished our portions, the crispy crust that had fallen on the table was gathered up carefully, crumb by crumb, to top off the delightful meal.

Today, when I pass a bakery and the aroma of fresh baked bread fills the air, my mind happily drifts back to Sunday morning, Six O'clock Mass, and Papa.

BREADS, BEVERAGES, CHEESE AND EGGS

FATHER DONAHUE'S SUNDAY NIGHT SUPPER

On Sundays we always looked forward to a visit from our friend, Father Donahue, director of the grand old Roman Catholic retreat house, Our Lady of the Oaks, in the picturesque little community of Grand Coteau, Louisiana. Father always came in the evening, after a retreat had ended, and consequently missed the main meal, which was always served at noon on Sunday. However, he was more than content with the light evening meal which, at the children's request, usually consisted of pancakes or French toast. Since both he and I were from New Orleans and fond of the traditional banana fritters made famous by Corinne Dunbar's Restaurant on St. Charles Avenue, it was only natural to slice a few bananas into the pancake batter. This soon became the customary Sunday night supper, to which Father Donahue looked forward with eager anticipation. When I make them, I think of those quiet Sunday evenings and stimulating conversations with a special friend.

BANANA PANCAKES

4 tablespoons cooking oil
2 well beaten eggs
1 cup milk
1 cup sifted flour
2 tablespoons brown sugar
¼ teaspoon salt
3 tablespoons baking powder
2 thinly sliced bananas
  Butter, powdered sugar or syrup

Combine oil, eggs and milk. Add sifted dry ingredients and beat until smooth. Add sliced bananas. Drop by large spoon onto hot griddle. As soon as edges begin to brown and center seems "settled", flip over. Watch carefully to avoid burning. Have platter warmed and place pancakes in stacks, with a pat of butter in between. Dust with powdered sugar or serve with syrup.

Makes 12 medium pancakes

Carol Ann Roberts Dumond

BREAKFAST BRAN MUFFINS

2 cups All Bran cereal	2½ teaspoons soda
1 cup 40% bran cereal	½ cup shortening
1 cup boiling water	2 eggs
2¾ cups flour	½ quart buttermilk
½ teaspoon salt	1 cup pecans
2 cups sugar	Blueberries or raisins

Pour hot water over cereal. Mix and cool. Sift together flour, salt and soda. Cream sugar and shortening. Beat eggs. Add buttermilk, sugar mixture and pecans. Stir well. Fill muffin tins ½ full. Add 8 raisins or blueberries and fill muffin tins ⅔ full. Bake 20 minutes at 325 degrees.

3 dozen muffins

Can be refrigerated 2 weeks

Charles Bernard, Jr.

BREAKFAST SQUARES

8 slices bread (crusts removed)	2½ cups milk
1 pound sausage, browned	½ teaspoon prepared mustard
¾ pound grated cheddar cheese	1 can cream of mushroom soup
4 eggs	¼ cup water

Break bread into pieces and place in bottom of 9 x 13 pan. Layer sausage, then cheese. Beat eggs, milk and mustard and pour over layers. Mix soup and water and pour over all. Bake at 300 degrees for 1 hour.

Nancy Northcutt

A NEW BABY

Perhaps it sounds strange, but cinnamon rolls are symbolic to me of a wonderful moment in my life—and inspire special memories of my mother and dad, my grandmother, and the miracle of birth. I recall my mother presenting little gifts to my sister, Cathy and me, then—perhaps it was late evening or maybe early morning— leaving for the hospital. We knew there would soon be a new baby in the family and were too excited to sleep. At about six a.m., my grandmother asked us to "help her" make cinnamon rolls. We put on aprons that had been tied under our arms (I was ten and Cathy was nine) and dove right in. Around 6:30, the phone rang, and my grandmother answered it, even though my sister and I made a dive for it. "Girls," she said, "your father has something to tell you." We both got on the phone,

CINNAMON ROLLS

Bread
- 1½ cups water
- 1 teaspoon salt
- ½ cup sugar
- 4 tablespoons shortening
- 1 package dry active yeast
- 1 egg
- 5 cups flour (about)

Put yeast, 2 tablespoons sugar, ½ cup warm water into small bowl. Let stand about 10 minutes. In a larger bowl (2½ quarts), put all other ingredients, but not all the flour. Beat well. Add the yeast mixture and flour enough to make a kneadable dough. Knead for about 10 minutes. Put in a warm place to rise - it will double in bulk. Turn on floured board and roll thin - take a sizable amount to make first rolls. A larger amount will be too large to handle.

Filling:
- 1 stick melted butter
- 1 cup sugar
- 2 tablespoons cinnamon

Spread with melted butter, sugar and cinnamon. Roll like jelly roll and cut for rolls. Let rise until soft to touch. Bake in 375 degree oven for 35 to 40 minutes. Remove from pan immediately. (Always put dough in greased pan).

Esther C. Bell (Gaga)
Christy Bell Zanazzi

and Dad told us that we had a baby sister, named Jane Margaret. Needless to say, those cinnamon rolls were the best we ever had, and memories of that morning are among my most precious ones.

CREAM SCONES

2 cups flour
4 teaspoons baking powder
½ teaspoon salt
2 teaspoons sugar
4 tablespoons butter

2 eggs, well beaten (except for a small amount of egg white)
½ cup whipping cream (but do not whip)

Mix the first four ingredients and cut in butter. Add eggs and cream. Roll to ¾ inch thickness. Cut out with biscuit cutter or cut in squares. Brush with saved egg white. Bake on ungreased baking sheet at 425 degrees for 12-15 minutes. Serve split and buttered or with cream cheese and strawberry jam.

Makes about 2 dozen

Mimi McGlasson Francez

FRENCH TOAST

10-12 slices stale French bread
5 eggs
2 teaspoons vanilla

½ cup sugar
Cooking oil
Confectioner's sugar

Slice the French bread before it is stale; otherwise the crust crumbles and the bread slices lose the crust. Mix eggs, vanilla, and sugar. Place one slice of stale bread in the egg batter until the bread has "soaked up" the batter, about 15 minutes. Then fry the soaked slices on hot, oiled griddle. Fry the bread about 2 minutes on each side. Remove and sprinkle with confectioner's sugar and serve while warm.

Carol Ann Roberts Dumond

PAIN PER DU OR "LOST BREAD"

12 slices stale bread
1 cup sugar
4 eggs

1 teaspoon vanilla
¼ cup milk

Beat sugar and eggs together, add vanilla and milk. Dip stale bread in egg mixture. Fry on hot black skillet covered with oil. Top with butter and powdered sugar.

Serves 4-6 people

Dale Doucet

CAJUN BREAKFAST

Couche-Couche has long been a Cajun breakfast favorite. It is simply corn meal, water and salt cooked in a well-greased iron skillet and served with Caillet (clabber) and syrup. There was a time when this simple breakfast was a matter of economic necessity. Today, many people consider it a real treat.

COUCHE-COUCHE

¼ cup vegetable oil
2 cups corn meal
¾ cup flour
1 tablespoon baking powder
1 teaspoon salt
1 cup water
½ cup milk

Heat oil in 10" black iron pot. Mix all dry ingredients. Add water and milk - being sure it is not too dry (it will be thick). Put into hot oil, cover to steam and form a crust (about 10 minutes). Uncover and stir, and break into small pieces. Lower heat, stir frequently while cooking the next 15 minutes. Serve with cold milk as a cereal.

4 servings

Bettie J. Baque

LOU'S CORN BREAD

When I was a little girl, there was nothing more special than going to my grandmother's house. Today, it is just as special. We are richly blessed, because Ma is still with us at the age of 93. Visits are still filled with fun and good food. When we arrive, there is always a pot of fresh peas and a pan of corn bread on the stove, as there was in my childhood. But this is not just any corn bread; it is LOU'S CORN BREAD. Lou has been helping my grandmother for over half a century, and I've tried lots of corn bread since I first tasted hers as a child. I firmly believe that Lou, who is now 70 years old, still makes the best corn bread in Louisiana—or anywhere else, for that matter. It is a rare taste treat and always a reminder of happy childhood days, spent with these two wonderful women.

MEXICAN CORN BREAD

2 eggs
½ teaspoon baking powder
1 cup buttermilk
⅓ cup oil
2-4 chopped jalapeño peppers

2 tablespoons chopped bell peppers
½ cup chopped green onions
1 ½ cups self-rising corn meal
1 cup cream style corn
1 cup grated cheddar cheese

Mix everything together except cheese. Pour half batter in pan. Sprinkle half cheese and pour rest of batter, then the rest of the cheese. Bake at 450 degrees for 30 minutes.

Connie Voth

SPINACH TOPPED FRENCH BREAD

1 stick melted butter
8 ounces grated cheddar cheese
8 ounces grated mozzarella cheese

1 box frozen chopped spinach, thawed and well drained of liquid
Garlic powder to taste
1 loaf French bread, split in half lengthwise

Mix all ingredients except French bread thoroughly. Spread mixture uniformly on cut surface of French bread. (May be wrapped in foil and frozen at this point). Bake on cookie sheet at 350 degrees for 10 to 15 minutes or until bubbly.

Serves 8.

Daynese Haynie

ZUCCHINI BREAD

1 cup biscuit mix
1 small finely chopped onion
½ teaspoon salt
½ teaspoon seasoned salt
½ teaspoon oregano
½ cup Parmesan cheese

Red pepper or Tabasco
2 tablespoons chopped parsley
1 mashed clove garlic
½ cup vegetable oil
4 eggs, slightly beaten
3 cups thinly sliced zucchini

Mix all ingredients together, adding zucchini last after other ingredients are well mixed. Bake at 350 degrees for 25 minutes in a greased oblong 13 x 9 x 2 pan.

Mary Thibeaux

MILDRED'S KITCHEN COUNTER

Probably every person who was allowed to "help" with the cooking as a child has special memories of those times. Among mine is the memory of gathering with my siblings while our baby-sitter, Mildred, made biscuits. She would turn the task into entertainment for us.

Mildred began by rolling out the dough on the floured kitchen counter and making careful circles with the cookie cutter. But the real fun began when she reached the last corner of the square of the dough, and a twinkle in her eye signaled that our turn was at hand. She would cut overlapping circles to make crescent-shaped "Moon Biscuits," and that was the cue that we were free to collect the remnants and let our imaginations guide our hands as we fashioned such fanciful treats as Clown Biscuits, Flower Biscuits and Snake Biscuits. Our biscuits may have tasted the same as the circular biscuits our parents ate, but I think that the extra ingredients of fun and fancy made them a little special.

DOUBLE V BISCUITS

2 cups all-purpose flour
¼ cup shortening
1 teaspoon salt
1 tablespoon baking powder
¾ cup buttermilk

Preheat oven to 450 degrees. Mix flour, shortening, salt and baking powder until coarse. Add buttermilk and mix until dough is soft. Place dough on a floured surface and roll about ½ inch thick. Cut biscuits to preferred size and place in a greased pan and cook about 12 to 15 minutes.

About 1 dozen biscuits

Always use high quality shortening and do not handle biscuits too much, as this will make them tough.

Linda Villard Supple

Play-Doh had been banned in our house after significant quantities of it mysteriously appeared between the keys of the piano, but we considered Mildred's biscuit dough even better. Certainly, the memories are.

FROM SCRATCH

"Mr. Claude" was a carpenter who, with his son, was involved in remodeling our house in Lafayette. He had a five-year-old grandson, the apple of his eye, and he always wanted the little boy to spend Friday nights at his house. The youngster was less than enthusiastic, because at his home he could watch Saturday morning cartoons, while at Paw Paw's he might very well be put to work instead. In an effort to provide an inducement that the child couldn't refuse, Mr. Claude promised one Friday that if his grandson came home with him, "Maw Maw will make

EASY "HOMEMADE" BISCUITS

3 cups biscuit mix
1½ cups milk
¼ cup mayonnaise
3 tablespoons oil

Preheat oven to 375 degrees. In medium size bowl, stir together biscuit mix, milk and mayonnaise. Stir only until all dry ingredients are mixed in. Place a sheet of freezer wrap on counter (for easy clean-up). Sprinkle generously with an additional cup of biscuit mix. Scrape out biscuit dough onto sheet. This dough will be very wet. Sprinkle biscuit (mix) on hands and top of dough. Work very gently with your hands just until dough can be handled and press out flat approximately ½ inch thick. Cut with round biscuit cutter which has been dipped in biscuit (mix). Place oil in baking pan (I use a cookie sheet with a rim around the edge). Flip each biscuit in oil so that top is oiled. Place in pan, but not quite touching. Bake 12 minutes at 375 - 400 degrees or until lightly browned on top.

Approximately 12 - 3 inch biscuits

Growing up, we always had "homemade" biscuits made "from scratch". This is an easier and quicker version for those wonderfully crisp and succulent biscuits we had then.

Bettye Walker

home-made biscuits from scratch Saturday morning."

He saw interest in the boy's eyes and waited expectantly for an affirmative answer. He got a question instead. "Paw Paw, how does she scratch them?"

Most families observe holiday traditions that are uniquely their own, passed down through generations. This is important in my family, and certain recipes are part of family tradition. I do not know many people who consider biscuits an essential part of the Easter celebration. But when I was young, a part of the observance that I looked forward to most eagerly was the time when my Grandmother would bake Easter

EASTER BISCUITS

5 pounds flour
2½ cups sugar
1½ cups sesame seeds
2 tablespoons anise seed
1 teaspoon salt
2 cups melted butter
1 cup shortening
2 packages yeast
½ cup warm water
2 beaten eggs
4½ cups scalded milk

Mix flour, sugar, sesame seed, anise seed, and salt. Blend well. Add melted butter and shortening to flour mixture, mix well. Add yeast that has been dissolved in warm water. Next, add eggs and milk, knead. Don't knead the dough too much or it will toughen the biscuits. Let rise until double in size. Form dough into golf ball size balls. Flatten the balls of dough and place on an ungreased baking sheet. Cover and let rise about one half size. Bake on middle rack of oven, 400 degrees for 15 minutes or until light brown.

Glaze:
½ pint whipping cream
1 cup sugar

Over medium heat, stir whipping cream and sugar until sugar is thoroughly dissolved. Do not overcook. Let glaze cool. Brush tops of hot biscuits with glaze.

Biscuits may be prepared ahead of time. May be served warm or cold. They freeze well.

Carol Goings

Biscuits, following a recipe that has been in our family for generations. Today, at Easter Time, I wait just as eagerly for my mother to prepare this special family treat. It is a link with the past that is very precious. (And, Easter Biscuits are delicious.)

GRANDMA ELOZIA'S UPSIDE-DOWN CORN BREAD

Corn bread was a regular part of our daily meals. Rarely did we not have a fresh corn bread for supper. On Saturday nights and Sunday mornings my Mom would bake white or "light" bread for the Sunday meal. In the late spring and early summer, when the corn supply was low, we had "light" bread, made from flour, fairly regular.

My grandma's corn bread was the best I have ever eaten. She would make what was commonly called "un pain d'mais tourne'," or upside-down corn bread. This bread was baked in a large black skillet on top of the wood stove. Halfway through the baking the bread was turned over in the skillet and finished. This method produced a corn bread with a great hard crust on the top as well as on the bottom.

Now, my grandma had a unique way of serving her corn bread. She would serve it in a bowl of milk. However, she insisted on boiling her milk. She would do so in a large black cast-iron pot. She had a way of boiling the milk so that it would have a burnt taste. Somehow, during the boiling, there was a part of the milk that would stick to the bottom of the pot. That part would scorch and thus would give the rest of the milk a burnt taste. When I was there, I loved it when she would let me scrape the bottom of the pot. I still remember the taste of this wonderful mixture of hot upside-down corn bread in warm burnt-flavored milk. I would pay dearly for an earthen-ware bowl of Grandma Elozia's corn bread and milk.

Floyd Sonnier

WAFFLES

The sound of an electric mixer on Sunday morning brings back some of my most beautiful memories. Sunday was the highlight of the week in my childhood. I would awaken to the mixer's sound as my Dad assumed his once-a-week role as Chef. That twirling sound of the mixer announced that he was making waffles from scratch—to be served with crisp bacon and orange juice. A wonderful Sunday morning meal, and, afterward, a family together—going to church. A special memory.

CAJUN CRAWFISH CORNBREAD

2 cups cornmeal
1 tablespoon salt
1 teaspoon baking soda
6 eggs
2 medium chopped onions
½ cup chopped jalapeño peppers

16 ounces grated cheddar cheese
⅔ cup oil
2 (16 ounce) cans cream style corn
2 pounds crawfish tails

In a large mixing bowl, combine cornmeal, salt and soda. In a medium bowl beat eggs thoroughly. Add onions, jalapeño peppers, cheese, oil, corn, and crawfish tails to beaten eggs. Combine this mixture with cornmeal mixture and mix well. Pour into greased 12 x 14 baking dish. Bake at 375 degrees for 55 minutes or until golden brown.

Cari Arcenaux

Acadiana Culinary Classic 1992 Le Petit Classique second place winner.

ZUCCHINI/PINEAPPLE BREAD

3 eggs
2 cups sugar
1 cup vegetable oil
2 teaspoons almond or vanilla extract
3 cups flour
2 teaspoons baking soda
1 teaspoon salt
½ teaspoon baking powder

1 ½ teaspoons cinnamon
1 ½ cups grated unpeeled zucchini
1 (8 ounce) can crushed pineapple, drained
1 cup chopped walnuts
1 (4 ounce) package instant vanilla pudding

Beat eggs, sugar, oil and extract until foamy. In separate bowl mix all dry ingredients. Combine with egg mixture and beat well. Add zucchini, pineapple, walnuts and instant pudding. Stir well. Pour into greased and floured bundt pan. Bake at 350 degrees for about 1 hour. Check with toothpick. Freezes well.

Kathleen V. Rudick

VEGETABLE BREAD

2 cans refrigerator biscuits
1-1½ sticks melted butter
½ cup chopped green
    peppers

½ cup chopped red peppers
1 cup Parmesan cheese

Preheat oven to 350 degrees. Cut biscuits into quarters. Sauté vegetables in half of the butter. Add rest of butter and toss in large bowl all ingredients to coat. Put into a bundt pan. Bake at 350 degrees for approximately 45 minutes. Turn out on a plate and let guests pull apart with their hands.

Red and green bell peppers make a very pretty bread, but use your imagination and add any vegetables you wish (onions and black olives are nice). May also alter this recipe for breakfast using cinnamon, sugar, brown sugar and pecans.

Nancy Landry

CITRUS TEA PUNCH

1½ cups water
1 tea bag
1½ cups orange juice
1½ cups pineapple juice
½ cup lemon juice

1 cup sugar
3 cups chilled ginger ale
  Orange or lemon slices
  (optional)

Bring water to a boil in a large saucepan, add tea bag. Remove from heat, cover and let stand 5 minutes. Remove tea bag. Add fruit juices and sugar, stirring until sugar dissolves. Chill. Stir in ginger ale just before serving. Add slices of fruit, if desired.

2 quarts

Cheryl Ottinger

DAD'S LIQUEUR

In 1964, after my Dad died, I was cleaning out his old desk, finding things that provoked poignant memories, when I came across his recipe for Cherry Bounce. It brought back a flood of vivid memories, because when Dad made the delicious liqueur, it was always a special day.

Somehow the Cherry Bounce was symbolic of closeness in the family, particularly with my Dad. And, of course, the taste of the delicious drink was vivid in my mind and taste buds.

The recipe stayed on my mind, and a year later I felt compelled to use it. I had no problem gathering all the necessary utensils, because I could see them in my mind as Dad had worked with them.

After that, I gathered up Mama and all the kids and we drove from our home in Patterson to the French Market in New Orleans, where we purchased a case of dark Bing cherries just off the tree. Back home on the Atchafalaya River, the kids all joined in mixing the brew, as I had with my father. We finished it and put it away until just before Christmas. When we checked it, the cherries had sunk to the bottom, and it was tasting time. We siphoned a liqueur glass full and passed it around. It was as delicious as my memories.

CHERRY BOUNCE

10 quarts cherries (Bing)
5 pounds sugar
½ pint brandy
7-8 fifths straight bourbon whiskey

In a demi-john (5 gallon size) measure cherries one quart at a time. Pinch each cherry to break the skin (do not mash) over a funnel so juice will be saved. Add sugar one-half pound per quart of cherries. Shake container so sugar falls through cherries. Add one-half pint of brandy, then add bourbon until it reaches bottom of the neck of the demi-john. (Use inexpensive straight bourbon, do not use a blended bourbon). With a ⅜ inch dowel wood rod that reaches bottom, stir mixture until sugar is dissolved. Place a cork on top with a wine breathing tube through cork. Place in a dark cool place.

Start cherry bounce when new cherries come in, in June or July. They will float until just before Christmas, then they will sink to the bottom. Get a siphon and taste the most delicious liqueur.

Bill Kenny
Lydia Patin Beaullieu

GRANDMOTHER'S RECIPE

This unusually thick and rich recipe is from Bastrop, Louisiana, where my family is from. Its distinctive thickness identifies the nog to anyone familiar with the recipe, and when I go to Christmas parties in New Orleans or other cities in the state and find this egg nog, I know that there must be someone at the party with a Bastrop connection. My grandmother gave this recipe to my mother when my parents got married.

EGG NOG

Per person:
- 1 egg
- 1 tablespoon sugar
- 1 tablespoon bourbon (use the good stuff)
- Whipping cream (½ pint is about right for 8 eggs)
- Nutmeg

Separate the eggs, beat the yolks, and add the sugar gradually, continuing to beat. DRIP the bourbon into the mixture, beating constantly. Beat egg whites until stiff. Fold into yolk mixture. Whip the cream and add to rest. Spoon into glasses and dust with nutmeg if desired.

The yolks, sugar, and bourbon can be done in advance but the whites and cream must be added at the last minute or the egg nog will separate. If you find that the nog has separated when you are ready to serve, you can either fold it back together or just use the big ladle that you're going to use to serve it to gently mix everything back together.

David V. Snyder

CAJUNS & COFFEE

Talleyrand, who was Napoleon's agent in the transaction called The Louisiana Purchase, once described good coffee as "black as the devil, hot as hell, pure as an angel and sweet as love." Dr. Vincent Marino, long-time editor of the Lafayette, Louisiana Daily Advertiser, wrote, in a well-received national magazine article, that "South Louisianians have added '—and in the right cup, too'."

Cajuns like their coffee as described by Talleyrand, and they like it all day long. The coffee pot is always on the stove, and its contents are so strong that a newcomer to the area might be lifted off his feet by the first sip.

COFFEE MILK (CAFÉ AU LAIT)

¼ cup coffee
¾ cup milk (heated very hot, but not boiling)
½ teaspoon sugar (or to taste)

Pour together and stir.

1 cup

Elaine Mann

There is a protocol to the drinking of coffee in Cajun Country, as there should be with something which is at the very heart of the culture and life-style. The coffee doesn't vary in strength or temperature, but the vessel in which it is served does—and is very important to the coffee drinking ritual. Cajuns "take" their coffee in ways that are clearly defined by custom. If asked for a small cup, don't offer a half a cup. A small cup means a demitasse, filled to the brim. Otherwise, a Cajun will ask for "a little bit in a big cup." Don't give him a demitasse. Give him a big cup with just a small taste. If he wants more, he'll ask for a half a cup. Or, he may ask for a small cup, "but only half." There's a distinction.

A "big cup" is not a usual request. It is usually the first cup of the day, after which a little in a big cup, or a half, or a half but in a small cup, or a small cup, is sufficient, if served up often enough.

In the sugar cane fields of Iberville Parish, some cane workers still carry a half-pint whiskey bottle into the field with them. But it is filled with coffee, not booze, and they sip it conservatively throughout the day.

Again quoting Dr. Marino, "In this picturesque land, no custom tells more about the people than those which surround the drinking of coffee."

GOLDEN MEMORIES

Golden Punch. Golden Memories. This wonderful concoction was introduced to my family at a cousin's wedding almost 40 years ago. We were so delighted that it became part of every important family occasion. We toasted my grandparents with it when they celebrated their Golden Wedding Anniversary. It was a solid hit with the guests at my wedding. We celebrated the christenings of both my children with the wonderful drink, and it has highlighted all our birthday parties and holiday gatherings. When I serve it, all those occasions are happily re-lived in my memory.

GOLDEN PUNCH

1 ½ cups sugar
3 cups water
3 cups prepared tea (room temperature)
3 cups unsweetened pineapple juice
1 ½ cups lime juice
1 (6 ounce) can frozen orange juice concentrate
3 cups chilled ginger ale

Mix sugar and water together. Cook over low heat until sugar is dissolved. Increase heat, cover, and boil for 5 minutes. Set aside to cool. Combine tea, pineapple juice, lime juice, and orange juice concentrate in large bowl. Stir to blend. Chill in refrigerator. When ready to serve, pour fruit mixture into punch bowl. Add sugar syrup and chilled ginger ale. Blend thoroughly.

3 quarts

Suzanne Miller

BREAKFAST IN A HURRY

1 (16 ounce) package bulk sausage
6 eggs
2 cups grated cheddar cheese
2 cups milk
1 cup biscuit mix
1 teaspoon parsley flakes
1 teaspoon chopped green onions
½ teaspoon season-all

Cook and drain sausage. Put in 8 x 11 inch casserole dish. Mix together thoroughly the remaining ingredients. Pour egg mixture over sausage and bake in 350 degree oven for 40 minutes.

Serves 10

Nancy Arceneaux

Acadiana Culinary Classic 1992 Le Petit Classique third place winner.

BREAKFAST OR BRUNCH CASSEROLE

1 pound hot breakfast
sausage
4 slices bacon
8 eggs
2 cups milk
1 teaspoon salt (or Tony
Chachere's seasoning)
1 teaspoon dry mustard
1 ½ cups Italian bread crumbs

1 cup grated cheddar cheese
½ cup grated Parmesan
cheese
3 tablespoons finely
chopped onion
½ teaspoon powdered or
granulated garlic
1 can drained, chopped
artichoke hearts (optional)

Brown sausage in frying pan and drain. Fry bacon, drain and crumble. Mix all ingredients together. Pour into 11 x 17 x 1 ½ inch or 13 x 9 inch casserole dish. Bake at 350 degrees for 45 minutes uncovered.

6-8 servings

Can be prepared the day before.

Felecia Lee

EASY HAM QUICHE

½ pound fresh sliced
mushrooms
2 tablespoons butter or
margarine
4 eggs
1 cup sour cream
1 cup small curd cottage
cheese

½ cup grated Parmesan
cheese
¼ cup all-purpose flour
6-8 drops Tabasco
2 cups (8 ounces) shredded
Monterey Jack cheese
½ cup chopped cooked ham

Sauté mushrooms in butter in a medium skillet until lightly browned; drain well and set aside. Combine next seven ingredients in an electric blender. In a large bowl, combine egg mixture, mushrooms, ham, and cheese. Pour into a 10 inch quiche dish. Bake at 350 degrees for 45 minutes or until top is firm. Let stand at least ten minutes before serving.

This can be served at room temperature also.

Margaret H. Trahan

COLLEGE CARE PACKAGE

The author who wrote "Real Men Don't Eat Quiche" obviously didn't know much about real men, or about quiche, or about either. Everyone in my home loves Quiche Lorraine, and when I prepare it, it calls up bitter-sweet memories: a time when I was so proud my children were in college, but a little sad when the weekends ended and they returned to their studies.

So that I could at least be assured of a place in their thoughts while they were away, I would prepare a dozen quiches at a time and freeze them. They were able to take back to college with them a little taste of Mama's home cooking, and a symbol of my love for them.

QUICHE LORRAINE

1   8 inch pie crust
4   slices crisp bacon, crumbled
4   thin slices onion, sautéed until soft
¼ to ½ cup finely chopped green onion
    tops
8   shredded paper thin slices ham
8   grated slices Swiss cheese
3   eggs
1   teaspoon Dijon mustard
1   cup whipping cream, heated
    Nutmeg
    Dash white pepper

Bake pie crust at 400 degrees for 15 minutes, until slightly brown. Put foil on top of crust as this may burn. Sprinkle the bacon and onion over the bottom of pie crust. Add ½ ham, ½ cheese and onion tops. Add rest of ham and cheese on top. Beat the eggs and mustard, add cream and continue beating. Pour over the ham and cheese etc. Let stand 10 minutes. Sprinkle a tiny bit of nutmeg on top. Bake at 300 degrees for 50 to 60 minutes.

Joan Miguez Blanchet

© FLOYD SONNIER '85
MARDI GRAS À LA POINTE NOIRE

"TEE-MAMOU TIM"

"Tee-Mamou Tim" symbolizes the entire joyful event surrounding Mardi Gras…from the rivalry to the pageantry, up to the midnight hour and the beginning of the Holy Season of Lent.

The colorful costumes, the wonderful lively Cajun music, the delicious spicy Cajun cuisine and the "joie-de-vivre" attitude embodies the whole Cajun culture.

This is what "Tee-Mamou Tim" is all about.

Floyd Sonnier

MARDI GRAS LA POINT NOIRE

From a distance, a cloud of dust rose above sounds of merriment. An accordion and a fiddle playing, in harmony, the melody of a Cajun Two-step. The horses, two by two, with colorful riders, their tall, pointed hats with streamers gently waving in the cool breeze, approached an anticipated excitement: "Garde-donc la-bas, les Mardi Gras viens!" "Look yonder, here comes the Mardi Gras!"

Mardi Gras (French for Fat Tuesday) is always celebrated the day before Ash Wednesday, in preparation of the beginning of Lent. It was, and still is, quite simply, the last big "fling" before settling down to forty days of fast, prayers and penance. At midnight on Tuesday, the celebration stopped.

"Courrir Mardi Gras" (running Mardi Gras) began early Tuesday morning when twenty-five to fifty or more men dressed in very colorful, homemade costumes with masks and tall, pointed hats (called Capuchons) banded together in a somewhat organized manner led by an "unmasked" leader, called "Le Capitan!" and blended fantasy with reality for the purpose of a fun-filled day when worries and cares were cast away.

The riders, all friendly neighbors and relatives, would leave from a designated place and circle their village in a slow pace to return to the starting point by late afternoon. Along their trip they would visit farm houses. Upon approaching someone's home, the "Captain," dressed in everyday clothes except for a purple cape and carrying a flag or a cow-horn, would ride ahead to the house and ask the farmer if he would welcome the "Mardi Gras." If the farmer agreed, and most did, the "Captain" would drop the flag or blow into the cow-horn signaling the band, waiting at the road, that they were invited. What a sight! Thirty, forty or so horses galloping full speed toward the house with colorful riders whooping and hollering was an excitement to see.

The "Mardi Gras" would entertain the farmer and his family by dancing and singing. They then begged for a reward. Some farmers would throw a live chicken to the crowd. The bank of men would then scramble to see who would catch the chicken. Sometimes they would receive a bag of rice or some pork sausage. They moved from farm house to farm house, collecting rewards for their entertainment. All this was carried back in a wagon following the group to town for a huge gumbo that night to feed everyone there. Musicians would come in to finish the night with a "fais-do-do" or dance, and at midnight, everyone went home.

The next day was Ash Wednesday and the beginning of Lent.

Floyd Sonnier

GUMBOS, SOUPS, SALADS AND SALAD DRESSINGS

First You Make a Roux

Like most youngsters, I was constantly underfoot when Mom was cooking something I particularly liked. I wanted to help with everything, and I enjoyed it all—until the time when she finally gave in and let me stir the roux. At first it was delightful watching the thick wheat flour change color as I wielded the wooden spoon in the black iron pot. After a while, however, my arm began to grow weary. When it actually began to ache, I asked Mom to take it over. It was then that I learned the basic rule: when you begin stirring a roux, you keep going until it is just right—even if your arms threatens to fall off, the phone rings, the doorbell sounds, or the world caves in.

Basic Roux

⅔ cup flour
¾ cup oil

Mix the flour and oil in a heavy iron pot until it is thoroughly mixed before you turn on the fire under the pot. After it is mixed, turn the fire on medium to low, stirring constantly. Stir all over the bottom of the pot to be sure that no particles stick to the bottom. As you stir, the roux browns slowly. Don't cook your roux fast, because as it reaches the done point, it will be too hot and burn. When your roux is a rich dark brown, turn off the heat immediately, continuing to stir. Add water to lower the temperature slightly so the roux will stop browning. Or, you can add chopped onions and/or bell peppers to lower temperature. Continue stirring, return to heat and add the remainder of the ingredients for your stew or gumbo.

A heavy pot is a must to make a pretty roux. The heavier the pot, the easier your job will be. Before you start your roux, start heating water in kettle, the amount depending on whether you are making a gumbo or a stew. You must always add hot water to a roux. It is very important not to change the temperature of the roux by adding cold water to it. The measurements given above make a roux large enough for a stew with 1 hen, or a gumbo with two pounds of shrimp.

If you wish to make a larger recipe, enlarge the recipe in the same proportions given. We feel it to be important to use more oil than flour.

Mrs. Ronald Andrus

FILÉ

"Jambalaya, Crawfish Pie and a Filé Gumbo" go the lyrics to the Hank Williams classic. Filé is used to thicken gumbo. It is a powder made from sassafras. One writer notes that the Choctaw Indian word for sassafras is "Kombo." Could gumbo be of Choctaw origin? Who knows? Who cares?

CHICKEN AND CORNISH HEN GUMBO

    1 cup all-purpose flour
    3 quarts water or chicken broth
    ⅓ cup vegetable oil
    1 4½ pound frying chicken, skinned and cut
      into 8 pieces
    2 1¼ to 1½ pound Cornish hens, skinned and
      cut into 8 pieces
    2 medium chopped onions
    1 chopped clove garlic
    3 finely chopped green bell peppers
    4 chopped ribs celery
    1 tablespoon filé powder
    1 teaspoon concentrated crab and shrimp boil
      (or 1 teaspoon cayenne pepper, 1 bay leaf, 1
      teaspoon dried thyme)
    1 tablespoon salt
 1½ teaspoons freshly ground black pepper
    ½ pound coarsely chopped tasso, Cajun ham or
      smoked ham
    ½ cup finely chopped green scallion tops
    8 finely chopped sprigs flat-leaf parsley

To make the dry roux, heat a large black cast-iron skillet over medium-high heat, add the flour and stir constantly with a wooden spoon from the middle of the skillet outward until the flour is the color of cinnamon, about 30 minutes. Take the roux out of the skillet and set aside in a bowl. (You may make the roux ahead of time and store it, tightly sealed, in a jar or plastic bag in the freezer).

In a large casserole bring the water or broth to a

GUMBO

It is generally accepted that the Cajun favorite, Gumbo, is of African origin, and that the name stems from the African word for okra, which is traditionally used to thicken the savory dish. Gumbo is made with a roux (wheat flour browned in cooking oil—preferably in a black iron pot—while being stirred constantly until it is the exact right color), water, seasonings, and whatever a Cajun wants to put in it—usually shell fish, sausage, domestic fowl or wild fowl.

Gumbo was the staple of the early Cajun housewife. It could be prepared in advance, was economical, could be made from ingredients usually available around the home. And, if surprise guests showed up, she just added more water to the gumbo.

Chicken and Cornish Hen Gumbo *(continued)*

simmer over medium-high heat. In a large, heavy skillet heat the oil over medium-high heat until it is hot but not smoking. Lower the heat to medium and brown the poultry in the oil in batches until golden, about 3 minutes on each side. Drain the meat on paper towels and add it to the casserole of simmering water or broth. Drain all but three tablespoons of the oil from the skillet. Add the onions, garlic, peppers, celery and filé powder and cook over medium heat, stirring frequently, until the onions are soft, about 10 minutes. (The filé will become ropy at first, but will liquefy as it cooks).

Add the vegetables to the casserole and bring to a boil over medium-high heat. Put two cups of the simmering broth in a separate bowl, whisk in the dry roux a little at a time, continue to whisk until it is smooth. Add the roux mixture, a spoonful at a time, to the casserole, stirring until all the wet roux has dissolved and there are no lumps. Add the crab boil, salt, pepper and diced tasso. Reduce heat and simmer, uncovered, until the chicken and Cornish hens are tender, about one hour. Serve over rice and garnish with the chopped scallions and parsley.

Let guests add filé powder and hot sauce to taste.

12 servings

Kenneth Henke

GUMBO SEASON

I grew up as a "military brat," moving often, and living all over the world. During this time in my life, I enjoyed many exotic dishes in exotic places, but possibly my most memorable culinary treat came in the small Cajun town of Scott, Louisiana.

It was Gumbo Season, and a special friend had issued an invitation to dinner which was eagerly accepted, because her cooking was *très magnifique*. Arriving at her home, we were greeted by the delicious smell of gumbo, shown the pot, and told "help yourselves."

I had never seen anything like the gumbo. There were turkey necks in it, and what I thought was chicken. It was incredibly delicious, and probably marked the point at which I truly became a Cajun—not by birth but by choice. Cajun cooking always provides a few surprises. This one: what I thought was chicken turned out to be home-grown pigeon. Again, *très magnifique*.

PIGEON AND TURKEY NECK GUMBO

    5 pigeons, plucked and cleaned
    5 turkey necks cut into 2 inch
      pieces
    2 chopped onions
    1 chopped bell pepper
    1 stalk chopped celery
 1 ½ cups flour
    1 cup oil
      Salt and pepper to taste
      Water
      Rice

First you make your roux! Cook flour and oil in large pot until dark brown. Add vegetables and sauté. Add about 1 gallon of warm water, let simmer until roux has dissolved. Add meat and heat until it starts to boil. Cook at a slow boil for about 1 ½ to 2 hours, depending on toughness of birds. You may have to add more water as it cooks depending on thickness of gumbo. Serve over rice.

Rose Landry

SHRIMP AND OKRA GUMBO À-LA-MOM-MOM

1 quart cooked okra or 1½ quarts fresh okra
4 tablespoons vegetable oil
2 tablespoons vinegar
1 medium chopped onion
1½ chopped bell peppers
1 clove minced garlic
1 small can tomato sauce
¼ cup cooking oil
1 large chopped onion
2 well minced garlic cloves
1 small can tomato paste
1 medium chopped bell pepper
1 tablespoon Worcestershire sauce
1 teaspoon sugar
Salt and pepper to taste
2 cups shrimp stock (Boil heads and shells in stock pot, which can be made ahead)
2 quarts of water
2 pounds fresh shrimp (without heads)

In a black pot or electric skillet, fry sliced okra in hot oil until slime is gone. Add vinegar, it will help cut slime - add onion, bell pepper, garlic, small can tomato sauce - cook covered about 30 minutes stirring well. In a gumbo pot or large pot, heat ¼ cup oil, add onion and garlic, sauté until golden brown over medium heat. Add tomato paste, bell pepper, Worcestershire sauce, sugar, cooked okra, salt and pepper. Cook uncovered for 5 minutes. Add shrimp stock along with 2 quarts of water (more if needed to keep it soup consistency) and stir well. Simmer 1 hour covered stirring occasionally. Add shrimp, cook 10 minutes more uncovered. Serve with rice, chopped green onions and parsley.

To make shrimp stock: 2 Knorr fish bouillon cubes with 2 cups boiling water or 2 can chicken broth - may be substituted for shrimp stock.

Serves 6

Bettie J. Baque

BROCCOLI CHEESE SOUP

1 box frozen chopped broccoli

1 large chopped onion

3 ribs chopped celery

1 stick butter or oleo

1 small jar of processed cheese

1 can cream of chicken soup

1 can cream of celery soup

2 soup cans of milk

Cook broccoli according to package directions and drain. Sauté onion and celery in butter until tender. Put broccoli, onion and celery into soup kettle and add cream of chicken soup, cream of celery soup, milk and processed cheese. Cook over low heat for about 30 minutes.

6 to 8 servings

Linzee Evans Langley

CORN AND CRAB SOUP

2-3 tablespoons bacon grease or margarine

6-9 ears fresh corn, cut off cob or 1 bag frozen corn

1 large chopped onion

1 medium chopped bell pepper

2-3 ribs chopped celery

1 bunch chopped green onions

1 pound peeled shrimp

1 pound lump crabmeat

3 cans cream of shrimp soup

Small amount of milk for thinning

Salt, red and black pepper to taste

Sauté in grease the corn, onion, bell pepper. When onion begins to clear, add the celery and green onions. Let these two wilt, then add the shrimp and crabmeat. Sauté until shrimp are pink. Add soup and small amount of milk to thin. Season with salt and pepper. Don't let soup boil. You want thick cream soup but you may need to add more milk.

Recipe is good doubled.

Nell Tolson

CORN & SHRIMP SOUP

4 cups fresh or frozen corn
  chopped slightly in
  blender or food processor
⅓ cup cooking oil
2 cups chopped onions
1 cup chopped celery
1 clove chopped garlic

1 (16 ounce) can stewed
  tomatoes, cut up or
  pureed in processor or
  blender
6 cups water
2 teaspoons Creole
  seasoning
4 teaspoons salt
  Tabasco to taste
3 cups peeled shrimp

Roux:

⅓ cup flour   ⅓ cup oil

Make Roux and set aside. Smother corn in cooking oil for about 30 to 45 minutes; add onion, celery, garlic and tomatoes. Let smother about 15 to 20 minutes longer. Add roux to smothered mixture. Add water, Creole seasoning, salt and Tabasco. Let cook 45 minutes to 1 hour. Add shrimp, cook until tender, about 3 minutes after it comes to a boil. Don't overcook shrimp.

1 gallon

Marie Dugas
Marguerite LeBlanc

CRABMEAT SOUP

½ tablespoon margarine
½ cup chopped onions
1 can tomato soup
1 can consommé
5 ounces of canned green
  pea soup (½ can)
1 cup half and half

¼ cup sherry
1 pound crabmeat
½ teaspoon garlic powder
½ teaspoon basil
  Dash of Worcestershire
  sauce
  Salt and pepper to taste

Sauté onions in margarine until soft. Add all other ingredients except crabmeat. Heat thoroughly and serve. This may be refrigerated and reheated when ready to serve.

Serves 6-10

Katie Flower

Acadiana Culinary Classic 1992 Le Petit Classique first place winner.

CREAM OF BROCCOLI SOUP

1 chopped onion
1 stick margarine
3 packages frozen, chopped broccoli
3 can cream of mushroom soup

2 cups milk
1 roll garlic cheese, sliced
1 roll jalapeño cheese, sliced
1 teaspoon Tony Chachere seasoning

Sauté onion in butter in a large pot until the onions are soft. Add broccoli and cover. Stir occasionally until the broccoli is tender. Stir in the remaining ingredients and serve hot.

Adam Trahan

Acadiana Culinary Classic 1992 Le Petit Classique second place winner.

CUBAN BLACK BEAN SOUP

1 pound black beans (dried)
2 quarts water
2 tablespoons salt
5 minced cloves garlic
½ tablespoon cumin
½ tablespoon oregano

1 ounce white vinegar
5 ounces olive oil
⅓ pound minced onions
½ pound minced bell peppers

Soak beans in water overnight. Add salt and boil beans until soft - crush garlic, cumin, oregano, and vinegar together. Heat olive oil adding onions, bell peppers and sauté until brown. Add crushed ingredients cooking slowly. Drain some water off of beans and add all ingredients together. Cook slowly for 20 minutes or until done. Serve with rice if preferred.

Serves 6

Charlotte Peck

CURRIED TOMATO BISQUE

½ cup finely sliced green onions
4 tablespoons melted butter
4 cans undiluted tomato soup

5 cups water
3 teaspoons curry powder (or more to taste)
3 egg yolks (grated - for garnish)

Sauté onion in butter until lightly browned. Add soup, water and curry. Heat thoroughly, stirring constantly. Serve hot or cold. Garnish with grated egg yolks.

8 to 12 servings

Lise Ann Baer

CUCUMBER CHILL

1 large chopped onion
4½ medium cucumbers,
  peeled and sliced
¼ cup melted margarine
¼ cup flour
5 cups canned chicken broth
2 bay leaves

½ cup sour cream
1 teaspoon salt
½ teaspoon dill weed
½ teaspoon hot sauce
1 cup half and half
2 tablespoons lemon juice

Sauté onions and cucumber in margarine until tender. Reduce heat and gradually add flour, stirring constantly. Cool 1 minute. Add broth and bay leave, stirring until it comes to a boil. Reduce heat and simmer 30 minutes. Pour into a blender and puree. Pour into a large bowl; add sour cream, salt, dill, and hot sauce. Cool and chill. Add half and half and lemon juice. Chill until very cold.

Robin Trahan

Acadiana Culinary Classic 1992 Le Petit Classique first place winner.

INN AT LITTLE WASHINGTON RED PEPPER SOUP

¼ cup olive oil
1 cup chopped onions
1 tablespoon fennel seed
¼ teaspoon thyme
½ bay leaf
½ teaspoon minced garlic
1 tablespoon chopped fresh
  basil
6 diced red bell peppers
2 tablespoons minced
  jalapeño pepper (seeds
  removed)

¼ cup flour
5 cups chicken stock
¼ cup chopped fresh tomato
  (peeled and seeded)
2 teaspoons tomato paste
½-1 cup heavy cream
  Salt and pepper to taste
  Sambuca liqueur
  (optional)

Heat olive oil over medium heat; add onions, fennel seed, thyme, bay leaf, garlic, basil, red bell peppers, and jalapeño peppers. Sauté over low heat until wilted, about 10 to 15 minutes. Add flour and cook for 10 minutes, stirring constantly. Add chicken stock, whisking until smooth, along with the tomatoes and tomato paste. Cook soup over medium heat, partially covered, for 45 minutes. Puree in a blender or food processor. At this point, soup can be frozen for future use. When ready to serve, add cream and simmer for 10 minutes. Just before serving, adjust seasonings and add a splash of Sambuca.

Sambuca (Great in demitasses before dinner).

Suzanne Odom

AROMA OF HALLOWEEN

It is remarkable how the aroma of different foods calls up special childhood memories. When I smell homemade vegetable soup simmering on the stove, I immediately think of the joy that Halloween brought to me as a child.

In our home, that aroma was signal that the time of ghosts, goblins and things that go bump in the night was at hand. Every Halloween, my mother's vegetable soup would be waiting when I arrived home from school with my brother and sisters. It had been simmering all day. It was a special treat, but also my mother's loving way of helping us to stay warm as we went about the neighborhood on our happy mission of Trick or Treat.

HEALTHY VEGETABLE SOUP

1 large coarsely chopped bell pepper
3 stalks chopped celery
1 small chopped bell pepper
1 large bay leaf
3 beef bouillon cubes
1 large can chopped tomatoes
1 small can tomato sauce
  Salt, pepper and Tony Chachere's seasoning to taste
1 large round steak (cut into 1 inch pieces)
5-6 large sliced carrots
1 (16 ounce) bag frozen corn
1 (16 ounce) bag frozen green beans
1 (16 ounce) bag frozen chopped okra
2 small cubed potatoes
⅓ small cabbage (cut into 1 inch pieces)
4-5 quarts water

add onions garlic

In a large soup pot boil water, meat, bay leaf and seasoning until meat is almost tender (about 1 hour). Add remaining ingredients and simmer for 2½ hours until well done.

Laurie Martin Smith

LUMP CRABMEAT AND ARTICHOKE HEART BISQUE WITH SMOKED RED BELL PEPPER SAUCE

Bisque:

4 tablespoons butter
4 tablespoons flour
2 cans artichoke hearts, chopped, reserve liquid
1 ½ cups rich seafood stock
1 cup (½ pint) heavy whipping cream
1 cup milk
1 pound lump white crabmeat
Fresh basil (approximately 8 leaves)
1 teaspoon seasoned salt
Few dashes white pepper
Few dashes hot sauce

In your favorite heavy soup pot, melt butter and add flour and stir constantly for two (2) minutes. Add reserved artichoke liquid, stock, whipping cream and milk, stirring between each addition. Add basil, salt, pepper and hot sauce. It is imperative that fresh basil is used. Gently stir in chopped artichoke hearts and crabmeat. Top with Smoked Red Bell Pepper Sauce in the design of your choice.

Sauce:

1 red bell pepper
2 tablespoons olive oil

Take one red bell pepper and place on charcoal grill or under oven broiler. When skin is charred, place in a paper bag for approximately 10 minutes. Remove skin and seeds and place flesh in a blender with two tablespoons of olive oil and process until smooth. Place sauce in a squeeze bottle and swirl on the top of each individual bowl or in a tureen for an elegant look.

This recipe was a 1991 gold medal winner in The Times of Acadiana cooking contest!

Charlinda D. Hebert

MEATBALL SOUP

3 tablespoons olive oil
2 cloves minced garlic
2 ounces chopped ham
½ cup chopped parsley
1 large sliced onion
½ teaspoon dried basil
1 (15 ounce) can tomatoes

3 tablespoons tomato paste
4 cups chicken broth
1 pound small meat balls
 (1-inch in diameter,
 cooked and drained)
 Fresh grated Parmesan
 cheese

Add any of the following:

3 leeks, white part only
1 large chopped potato
2 small sliced zucchini
1 cup cauliflower florets
1 cup peas
½ cup sliced mushrooms

2 sliced carrots
1 (10 ounce) package Italian
 green beans
1 can lima beans or red
 beans

Heat oil in Dutch oven or large kettle. Add next 5 ingredients and sauté until onion is soft and golden. Add tomatoes, tomato paste and stock. Reduce heat and simmer, uncovered, 30 minutes. Correct seasoning. Base may be frozen at this point. Add remaining ingredients as desired, starting with those that require longest cooking time, such as potatoes, carrots, cauliflower and beans. When partially cooked, add other ingredients. Be careful not to overcook. Serve hot, sprinkle with freshly grated Parmesan cheese. If too thick, add more stock.

Barbara Bills

OYSTER AND BRIE SOUP

3 dozen small to medium oysters in their liquor
4 cups cold water
½ pound unsalted butter
¼-½ cup flour
1 cup coarsely chopped onion
½ coarsely chopped celery
½ teaspoon white pepper
½ teaspoon ground red pepper

1 pound fresh Brie cheese, cut in small pieces with rind on
2 cups heavy cream
½ cup champagne, optional
½ bunch chopped green onions
1 small handful of finely chopped tasso
½ pound bacon, fried and crumbled

Combine oysters and water together and refrigerate for 1 hour. Strain and reserve the oysters and water. In a large skillet melt the butter over low heat. Add the flour and beat with a metal whisk until smooth. Add the onions and celery; sauté about 3 minutes, stirring occasionally.

Stir in the peppers and sauté about 2 minutes and set aside. In a 4 quart saucepan, bring the oyster water to a boil. Stir in the sautéed vegetable mixture until well mixed. Turn heat to high. Add cheese; cook until cheese starts to melt, about 2 minutes, stirring constantly. Lower heat to a simmer and continue cooking for about 4 minutes stirring constantly. Remove from heat, strain soup and return to pot. Turn heat to high and cook about 1 minute stirring constantly. Stir in cream; cook until close to a boil, about 2 minutes. Add green onions and champagne if desired. Lower heat and add the oysters and handful of tasso. *Check the seasoning at this point and add red pepper and salt to taste. When oysters curl serve immediately in bread bowls with crumbled bacon to garnish the top.

Margaret LaBorde

POTATO SOUP

5-6 large Irish potatoes
1 sliced large onion
Salt, black pepper & garlic powder to taste

½ pound grated cheddar cheese
1 quart milk
Chopped green onions to garnish

Peel and dice potatoes and onion. Boil in 5 quart pot with enough water to cover by an inch. Season water with salt, black pepper and garlic powder. Once the potatoes are well cooked and water has been reduced, mash the potatoes, but keep a few large chunks. Add grated cheese (adjust amount: you don't want your soup to be too yellow in color). Add milk slowly until you get the consistency you desire. Adjust seasonings to taste. Green onions can be added to entire pot or garnish individual bowls.

Annette Bradley

TORTILLA SOUP

1 chicken (3 pounds)
5 quarts cold water
1 tablespoon ground cumin
½ cup fresh cilantro
1 tablespoon salt
1 large sliced carrot

3 sliced celery ribs
1 large chopped onion
1 ½ teaspoons coarse pepper
2 garlic cloves
2 teaspoons dried oregano

Garnish:
Monterey Jack cheese
Lime slices

3 cups fried tortilla strips
1 ½ cups avocado

Place all ingredients in a large stock pot. Bring to a boil and simmer, covered for 1 ½ to 2 hours. Remove chicken from broth. Remove meat from bones, and cut chicken into strips. Strain liquid, discard vegetables, and taste for salt.

When ready to serve, add to hot broth:
3 cups diced fresh tomatoes
2 cups chopped green onions

¼ cup fresh cilantro
Chicken

Serves 6 to 8

Lori Matthews

WHITE BEAN SOUP

3 tablespoons light
 margarine
1 medium chopped onion
2 stalks chopped celery
1 medium chopped bell
 pepper
1 pound smoked turkey
 sausage, sliced

1 (8 ounce) can tomato
 sauce
2 (15 ounce) cans Navy
 beans
1 (10 ounce) can chicken
 broth
2 cups water
 Salt free seasoning to taste

In heavy stock pot, sauté chopped vegetables in margarine. Add sliced sausage and tomato sauce. Simmer 15 minutes. Add beans (with juice), broth, seasoning and water. (Mash one cup of beans for consistency). Cook over medium heat for one hour.

6 to 8 servings

Delores Dugas

ZUCCHINI AND LEEK SOUP

2 tablespoons butter
1½ cups sliced leeks
4 cups chicken stock
1 pound cubed potatoes
2 tablespoons chopped
 parsley

½ teaspoon salt
2 medium zucchini, cubed
 Fresh ground pepper
½ cup heavy cream

Heat butter in a large saucepan. Add leeks and sauté over medium heat for 5 to 8 minutes. Add chicken stock, potatoes, parsley and salt. Bring to boil, reduce heat, cover and simmer for another 10 minutes. Stir in zucchini and continue simmering for another 10 minutes. Transfer to food processor or blender and puree. Return to saucepan, season with pepper and stir in cream. Serve warm or chilled.

8 servings

Tina Roy

CATALINA SALAD

1 head lettuce
1 medium chopped onion
3 chopped tomatoes
10 ounces grated cheddar
    cheese

1 can pinto beans
1 bottle Catalina dressing
1 medium bag Fritos
    Black olives - sliced for
    garnish

Chop lettuce and reserve for later. Wash and drain beans. Mix onion, tomatoes, beans and cheese together. Add bottle of salad dressing and toss all together. Chill several hours. Before serving add Fritos and lettuce and toss together. Garnish with sliced black olives.

8 servings

Lise Ann Baer

CHICKEN AND ARUGULA SALAD WITH BALSAMIC VINAIGRETTE DRESSING

Cubed cooked chicken
Chopped sweet red
pepper (1 tablespoon per
person)
Chopped pecans or
walnuts (1 tablespoon per
person)

Raisins (1 tablespoon per
person)
Leaves of arugula (or
roquette)

Dressing:

½ cup extra-virgin olive oil
2 tablespoons balsamic
    vinegar
1 whole clove garlic

½ teaspoon sugar
½ teaspoon salt
½ teaspoon fresh ground
    pepper

Combine ingredients for dressing in a jar. Cover and shake. Refrigerate until ready to use. Shake again before dressing salad. Toss pieces of cooked chicken, sweet red pepper, chopped pecans or walnuts, and raisins in dressing. Serve scoops on arugula leaves.

Vinaigrette dressings like this one are best if freshly made.

Betty Singleton Gaiennie

CONNIE'S WOP SALAD

1 large chopped tomato
10 chopped green stuffed
   olives
5 chopped black olives
1 tablespoon capers
2 chopped green onions

1 can chopped anchovies
½ fresh lime - juice
2 tablespoons olive oil
2 pods pressed garlic
   Iceberg lettuce, cored and
   broken by hand

Mix all ingredients, except iceberg lettuce in a large salad bowl. Refrigerate until ready to eat (about one hour). Mix iceberg. Salt and black pepper to taste. Serve immediately.

6 servings

Connie Galloway

FOUR STAR SALAD

⅔ cup heavy cream
1½ cups half and half
½ cup chopped green onion
½ cup chopped parsley
2 tablespoons chopped
   chives

Several leaves of any
   "pretty" lettuce
2 small sliced avocados
1 pound cooked asparagus
½ pound sliced mushrooms
1 (12 ounce) can sliced
   artichoke bottoms

Combine first five ingredients in a blender or food processor and blend until smooth. Chill at least one hour before serving on the side.

Line serving bowl with lettuce, the frillier and more colorful the better, because this is just for presentation. Combine remaining ingredients and arrange in bowl. Be sure to wait until just before serving to slice the avocado.

I like to rinse the artichoke bottoms to help remove the metallic taste from the can. If fresh asparagus is not available, use a tall can of asparagus spears, drained and cut in thirds. This salad is a big hit with men as well as ladies. It dresses up the simplest meal.

Serves six hungry or eight not so hungry

Jan Hamilton

FRUIT AND LIME SALAD

1 (3 ounce) package lime
  gelatin
1 cup boiling water
1 (6 ounce) can crushed
  pineapple

1 chopped apple
1 chopped banana
2 dozen red seedless grapes,
  halved
1 cup chopped pecans

Combine gelatin and boiling water to dissolve. Drain juice from pineapple and add enough cold water to make ¾ cup. Stir into gelatin and chill to consistency of egg whites. Add pineapple, apple, banana, grapes and pecans. Stir well and chill until firm.

Peggy A. Lee

LEMON SHRIMP PASTA SALAD

¼ cup white wine vinegar
3 tablespoons lemon juice
1½ tablespoons honey
1½ tablespoons chopped fresh
  ginger
1 tablespoon soy sauce
¹⁄₁₆ teaspoon cayenne pepper

1½ pounds large shrimp,
  peeled & deveined
12 ounces dry fettuccine
1 tablespoon Oriental
  sesame oil
⅓ cup chopped green onions
1 tablespoon lemon peel

In a 3 to 4 quart saucepan stir together first 7 ingredients. Place over high heat and bring to a boil stirring occasionally: cover and remove from heat. Let stand, stirring occasionally, until shrimp is opaque in center, about 10 minutes. Lift shrimp from pan with reserved liquid. Meanwhile, bring 3 quarts water to a boil in a 5 to 6 quart pan. Add fettuccine and cook, uncovered, over high heat until tender to bite, about 15 to 18 minutes. Drain and rinse under cold water. In a large bowl mix fettuccine, reserved cooking liquid, shrimp, sesame oil, onions and lemon peel until pasta is well coated. Serve or cover and chill.

Serves 4 to 6

Jeannie Simone

ORANGE AND RED ONION SALAD

1 medium red onion, thinly sliced
2 medium heads of green leaf lettuce (not iceberg, several heads of Boston lettuce may be substituted)
4 large naval oranges, peeled and sectioned without membranes
⅓ cup wine vinegar
1 teaspoon sugar
½ teaspoon salt
⅔ cup vegetable oil

Mix sugar and salt in vinegar until dissolved. Whisk in oil. Toss onion (add, as desired), lettuce and orange sections. Toss with enough dressing to coat. Serve immediately.

Beth Landry

TOMATO FETA CHEESE SALAD

2 cloves garlic
2 pints cherry tomatoes, halved
½ cup pitted ripe olives
1½ cups crumbled Feta cheese
¾ cup olive oil
½ cup and 2 tablespoons wine vinegar
1 teaspoon dried oregano
1 teaspoon dried thyme
Salt and pepper to taste

Rub salad bowl with garlic. Combine tomatoes, olives, and cheese in bowl. Combine rest of ingredients in jar and shake well. Pour over tomatoes. Refrigerate four hours.

Terri Foret

BLEU CHEESE SALAD DRESSING

⅓ cup salad oil
4 ounce package of bleu cheese
1 pint sour cream
Garlic powder to taste

Into a bowl, add oil and cheese; mash with a fork until you have desired consistency. Stir in sour cream, add garlic powder or any other seasonings you desire, stir and chill until you are ready to use.

It is best to make this dressing several hours before ready to use. If dressing is too thick, thin with milk.

Millie Talmon

HOMEMADE ITALIAN DRESSING

⅔ cup olive oil
⅓ cup red wine vinegar
2-3 cloves fresh garlic, pressed
2 tablespoons grated Parmesan cheese
2 teaspoons Italian seasoning
1 teaspoon dry or Creole mustard
1 dash Worcestershire sauce
1 dash Tabasco sauce
1 dash sugar
Salt
Pepper

Mix all ingredients in a container with a tight fitting lid and shake well. Can be stored in refrigerator - best allowed to sit at room temperature before tossing.

This is great on fancy leaf lettuce with fresh tomatoes, slivers of purple onion and lots of freshly grated Parmesan cheese.

Becky Berthelot

RASPBERRY SALAD DRESSING

⅓ cup extra virgin olive oil
⅔ cup canola oil
⅓ cup raspberry vinegar
6 teaspoons sugar
2 large cloves pressed garlic
¼ teaspoon salt

Mix ingredients. Serve over avocado and grapefruit slices with leaves of Bibb lettuce. Good with other salads, too.

Malise Foster

FLOYD SONNIER ©1987
"CLOPHAS THE CAJUN"

"ONE HUNDRED PERCENT TO GOD"

My dad, David, was a father of five and a loving husband who put God and his family above everything. He was a farmer and a carpenter for thirty-four years as a "share-cropper", as he did not own the land he worked. On a forty acre farm he grew cotton, corn and sweet potatoes. From his toil and sweat, he gave one-third to the landowner, two-thirds to his family and one-hundred percent to God. He was uneducated, but one of the wisest men I've known.

Floyd Sonnier

ONE HUNDRED PERCENT TO GOD!

My daddy was a farmer for in farming he knew to excel.
He worked the soil with endurance, sweat and a gentleness as well.

But more so he cultivated our lives with understanding and love,
and showed us patience, honor and an allegiance to our Lord above.

My daddy was a farmer, and he did best what he best knew how,
and from a small plot of land and the sweat off his brow,
he gave what he got from the dust and hard sod,
One-third to the man, two thirds to us,
and one hundred percent to God.

He taught us from the animals, the plants and the trees,
The beauty of God's nature and the desires to be free.

My daddy's simple wisdom would guide us through the years,
with love and laughter and sometimes a few tears.

Now I see my daddy getting old before his time,
for he struggled all his life for nickels and dimes.

And as the sun goes down in the evening of his life,
His reward lies in the lives of his children and his wife.

Floyd Sonnier

VEGETABLES AND SIDE DISHES

ROSA'S ARTICHOKE PASTA

¼ cup olive oil
⅓ cup chopped garlic
2 (6 ounce) jars artichoke hearts in olive oil
1 (12 ounce) package angel hair pasta

½ cup grated Parmesan cheese
½ cup grated Romano cheese
½ cup fresh chopped mint

Sauté garlic in olive oil until clear (be sure not to brown or scorch). Add artichoke hearts (cut in half). Boil pasta separately, drain thoroughly and add to mixture. Stir in Parmesan and Romano cheese. Top with freshly chopped mint.

Serves 6

Carla Gerami

BAKED BEANS

4 slices lean bacon, fried crisp
½ cup chopped onion
¼ cup chopped green pepper
½ cup ketchup
¼ cup brown sugar
¼ cup Worcestershire sauce

1 teaspoon barbecue seasoning (powdered) or ¼ cup barbecue sauce
1 teaspoon liquid smoke
1 teaspoon dry mustard
1 (31 ounce) can pork 'n beans, partially drained

In small skillet fry bacon, drain and set aside. Sauté onions and green pepper until wilted. In large bowl, combine ketchup, brown sugar, Worcestershire, barbecue seasoning, liquid smoke and dry mustard. Skim liquid from top of beans while still in can and remove fatty pieces of pork. Combine beans, bacon, onion, and peppers with other ingredients. Pour into a greased, 2 quart casserole. Bake at 350 degrees for 30 to 45 minutes.

6-8 servings

Rachelle Reichard

Most restaurants that serve the food peculiar to Acadiana will provide the hungry diner with a big helping of Red Beans and Rice any day of the week. But tradition in South Louisiana makes the culinary delight a "Monday meal." In the days before modern appliances, Monday was wash day among the people of Cajun Country, and it was pretty much an all day chore. SO…housewives put a pot of red beans on the stove early in the morning, and were able to forget about planning and cooking dinner while they took care of the family's laundry needs.

The tradition continues today. Some of us no longer look

CROCK POT RED BEANS

1 (16 ounce) bag dry red kidney beans
1 ham bone or bone-in ham hocks
1 large chopped bell pepper
1 large chopped onion
3 stalks chopped celery (leaves included)
1 small finely chopped carrot
1 tablespoon Tabasco or red pepper sauce
2 bay leaves
4 cloves crushed garlic
¼ teaspoon thyme
¼ teaspoon sage
¼ teaspoon marjoram
1 cup red wine
   Water to cover all ingredients
3 tablespoons garnish (chopped fresh parsley and green onions)
1 tablespoon salt
1 teaspoon white pepper
1 teaspoon black pepper
½ teaspoon red pepper

Put everything except the garnish in the crock pot on low heat. Cook covered for 6-10 hours. Check liquid level, adding water if needed to cover the beans. If there is too much liquid, turn the heat on high and leave the pot uncovered for a few minutes. Reduce heat for several hours or until ready to serve. Beans should be very tender. Remove bones and bay leaves and garnish before serving. Serve over rice with grilled or smoked sausage. May be frozen.

This recipe is more wholesome than some, since the vegetables are not sauted in oil. For an even leaner recipe, trim fat from ham, bring the ham to a boil on the stove top and allow to simmer for 10 minutes. Skim the oil from the surface, retaining the water to use in the recipe.

10 servings

Anne Simon

upon Monday as wash day. Many of us are able to stay home and tend those chores while casting an occasional eye on the pot. Usually, we crank up the washing machine as soon as the kids are in bed on Sunday night, and start the beans then. We awaken Monday to the wonderful aroma, and eagerly return in the evening to the delicious repast.

So Monday is still Red Beans and Rice day in many South Louisiana homes. The necessity is no longer there, but the tradition continues. And in today's complex world, we still need a pot that can't be forgotten.

PA-PO'S BAKED BEANS

8 slices bacon
1 large can pork and beans
1 medium diced onion
1 medium diced bell pepper
3 tablespoons dark Karo syrup
1 (10 ounce) bottle of Kraft barbecue sauce
1 tablespoon Worcestershire sauce
Dash of Tabasco
½ cup ketchup

Pan fry the bacon until tender. In a large bowl mix beans with bacon and drippings. Add the remaining ingredients and mix well. Pour mixture into a 9 x 11 x 2 inch casserole dish. Bake for 1 hour at 400 degrees uncovered.

The flavor of Kraft's barbecue sauce affects the taste, so you should only add Kraft!

Serves 10

Lynn Moroux

ORANGE BEET SUPREME

1 tablespoon cornstarch
½ cup sugar
¼ cup white vinegar
¼ cup frozen orange juice
  concentrate
2 tablespoons butter

¼ cup thinly sliced onions
2 (1 pound) cans baby
  beets, drained
2-3 (11 ounce) cans mandarin
  oranges, drained

Mix cornstarch and sugar. Stir in vinegar and orange juice concentrate. Stir until well mixed. Add butter, onions, beets and mandarin oranges. Put in covered 2 quart dish. Cook in oven at 325 degrees for 35 to 40 minutes.

Goes well with duck and other wild game.

Serves 6-8

Nancy Henke

GREEN STUFF

3 boxes frozen chopped
  broccoli
1 (16 ounce) jar Cheese
  Whiz

1 large chopped onion
1 stack crushed Ritz
  crackers
½ stick butter

Cook broccoli according to package directions, drain. Mix well with cheese and onion. Place in buttered 13 x 9 x 2 casserole. Melt butter, add crushed crackers, stir to coat. Sprinkle crackers over top of broccoli. Bake uncovered in 350 degree oven for 40 minutes.

This is an easy, but very good dish and a favorite of our entire family. The first time our 7 year old grandson tried it he came back for more asking, "Can I have some more green stuff?" Since that day we all call it the "Green Stuff."

10 to 12 servings

Lil Mitchell

CABBAGE ROLL CASSEROLE

1 pound ground turkey or
  other meat
1 large chopped onion
2 minced cloves of garlic
½ chopped medium bell
  pepper
1 can diced Rotel

1 cup water (add more as
  necessary) - can substitute
  V-8 juice
½ cup raw rice
  Season to taste
1 head shredded cabbage
  Grated cheddar cheese

Preheat oven to 350 degrees. Brown turkey and add onion, bell pepper, and garlic. Cook until vegetables are wilted. Drain meat mixture. Add can of Rotel, water and rice. Mix together well. Put shredded cabbage at bottom of 9 x 13 inch Pyrex dish. Pour meat mixture on top. Cover with foil and bake at 350 degrees for 1 hour. After baking, top with grated cheddar cheese and heat until melted.

Serves 4 to 6

Mimi McGlasson Francez

KATHERINE'S CABBAGE CASSEROLE

1 head cabbage
10 strips bacon
1 large can mushrooms
1 chopped onion

1 chopped bell pepper
¾ medium package Velveeta
  cheese
1 tablespoon Season-all

Preheat oven to 300 degrees. Boil cabbage. Fry bacon and let stand. Sauté onions, bell pepper and mushrooms in bacon grease. Add cooked cabbage and ½ crumbled bacon to sauté mixture. Sauté about 5 minutes. Add ½ cheese, seasoning and sauté another 5 minutes. Put in large casserole dish. Top with remaining bacon and cheese. Cover and heat for 30 minutes in 300 degree oven.

8 servings

Katherine Benson

CORN AND RICE CASSEROLE

1 stick margarine
½ cup small shrimp
½ cup finely chopped onion
½ cup finely chopped bell
   pepper
2 (11 ounce) cans of cream
   style corn

2 eggs, beaten
1 tablespoon sugar
1 ½ cups Minute rice
   (uncooked)
2 cups grated cheddar
   cheese
½ cup crabmeat

Sauté shrimp, onion and bell pepper in margarine. Add corn, eggs, sugar, uncooked Minute rice, crabmeat and ½ of grated cheese. Pour into greased square casserole and put remaining cheese on top. Bake 30 minutes at 350 degrees.

Casey Lee Doiron

Acadiana Culinary Classic 1992 Le Petit Classique first place winner.

GRANNY'S CORN PUDDING

2 well beaten eggs
1 chopped onion
1 chopped bell pepper
1 small jar pimentos

⅔ stick softened oleo
2 teaspoons flour
2 cans cream style corn

Preheat oven to 350 degrees. Lightly grease Pyrex dish. Mix all ingredients and bake until firm and golden brown or toothpick inserted in center comes out clean (approximately 30 minutes).

Deedie Beaullieu

BAKED CUSHAW

1 cushaw
2 cups water
3-4 cups sugar

1 block of butter
Apple pie spices

Peel and cut cushaw in 2 inch cubes. To four quart pot of cubed cushaw, add about 2 cups of water and 3 or 4 cups sugar. Steam covered until tender. Uncover and cook without mashing until about 1½ inches of liquid remains in bottom of pot. Pour in greased 2 inch deep flat casserole. Sprinkle top with apple pie spices. Top generously with butter (about 1 block). Bake until lightly brown on top in 325 degree oven.

I do the whole cushaw at one time and freeze in ziploc bags after cooking with sugar and water. When ready to use, place in a flat casserole, sprinkle top with apple pie spices, dot generously with butter, and bake.

Marguerite LeBlanc

PAPPY'S SMOTHERED OKRA

2 quarts freshly cut okra
¼ cup oil
3 chopped tomatoes

2 chopped onions
Salt and pepper to taste

Sauté all ingredients in heavy skillet over medium heat approximately 30 minutes. Season to taste.

Charles A. Barras, Jr.
Gina Rush Calogero

OFF THE COB

When people think of Cajun cooking, they usually think of meat, fish and fowl dishes, but no meal at our house was complete without at least two vegetables. Before Dad died, he kept a little garden that supplied us with tomatoes, bell peppers, onions, squash, peas and beans. After he passed away, we didn't keep up the garden, but there was a wonderful black man who came through the neighborhood in a horse-drawn buggy, selling fresh vegetables. My mother was undoubtedly one of his best customers.

Besides the green leafy vegetables she bought from him, Mom always demonstrated her loyalty to the local agriculture industry by serving Crowley rice and Opelousas yams. One or the other was a part of most meals. When she prepared many of the vegetable dishes Cajun style, like delicious Corn Macque Chou and Crawfish-Stuffed Bell Peppers, she always fixed a lot of

CORN MAQUE CHOUX

2 dozen ears of sweet corn
2 large chopped onions
¾ cup butter or margarine
2 tablespoons bacon grease
2 large chopped bell peppers
2 cloves minced garlic
1 small finely chopped hot chili pepper
1 medium finely chopped banana pepper
4 large chopped tomatoes (preferably home grown)
1 teaspoon Worcestershire sauce
¼ teaspoon Tabasco sauce
2-3 tablespoons flour or cornstarch
½ cup half and half cream
Salt and pepper to taste

Cut corn from cob. Melt butter in large heavy saucepan, add bacon grease. Sauté all chopped vegetables until wilted. Add tomatoes, Worcestershire sauce, Tabasco sauce, salt and pepper. Cook uncovered for 10-15 minutes on medium heat. Add the flour (or cornstarch) and cook 5 more minutes. Add the corn, half and half and cook for 15-20 minutes or until corn is tender.

Canned corn may be substituted for fresh corn.

10-12 servings

Marianne Schneider

vegetables the way her North Louisiana relatives did. I remember searching through boiling cabbage for the chunks of ham used for seasoning. And I remember having friends to dinner who had never heard of collard greens or tasted turnips.

While she prepared vegetables both Cajun and hill-country style, my mother would have nothing to do with her North Louisiana relatives' traditions in the preparation of seafood. "They don't know how to do it right," she always said, "but it's okay. They put Catsup all over it anyway."

SHRIMP-STUFFED MIRLITON

4 (8 ounce) mirliton squash
½ pound uncooked shrimp, peeled
½ pound coarsely chopped (cooked) smoked ham
1 chopped medium-sized onion
2 garlic cloves, minced
¼ cup finely chopped fresh parsley

¼ teaspoon ground thyme
¼ teaspoon ground hot red pepper
¼ teaspoon Tony Chachere's seasoning
11 tablespoons butter, cut into ½ inch bits
1 cup soft fresh crumbs made from French bread

Drop the mirlitons into enough boiling water to immerse them completely. Cook briskly, uncovered, for about 45 minutes, or until they show no resistance when pierced with the point of a knife. Drain the mirlitons and, when they are cool, cut them lengthwise into halves. Remove the seeds, and hollow out each half with a spoon to make boatlike shells about ¼ inch thick. Invert the shells on paper towels to drain. Puree the pulp. Transfer the pulp to a heavy ungreased skillet and, stirring constantly, cook over moderate heat until all of the liquid in the pan evaporates. Add 8 tablespoons of the butter bits to the puree and when it melts, stir in the shrimp, ham, onion, and garlic and continue cooking until shrimp are pink and onion is soft. Add parsley, thyme, red pepper, Tony Chachere's, and salt. Taste for seasoning. Spoon the shrimp-and-squash stuffing into the reserved mirliton shells, dividing it equally among them and mounding the tops slightly. Sprinkle the bread crumbs and the remaining 3 tablespoons of butter bits over the mirlitons. Arrange the shells in the buttered dish and bake in the middle of the oven for 30 minutes, or until the tops are brown. Serve at once.

Serves 8

Marguerite Smith

SUMMER VEGETABLES

I have a definite fondness for summer vegetables, and I owe this to my grandparents and the wonderful food memories they created for me each summer. Papa planted an enormous garden each spring which supplied the bounty for my grandmother's midday summer meals. In the Southern tradition of eating the main meal of the day at noon, Gage would call us to a dining room table that was laden with an array of fresh homegrown vegetables.

MIRLITON (VEGETABLE PEAR) DRESSING

3-4 fresh mirlitons (2 eggplants can be substituted)
½ pound ground pork
½ pound ground beef
1 pound ground ham
1 large finely chopped onion
3 finely chopped green peppers
1 can Rotel tomatoes
1 teaspoon Tony Chachere seasoning
1 teaspoon garlic powder
Salt
Italian bread crumbs

Peel vegetable pears (or eggplants), slice, and cook halfway submerged in water until soft. Drain the water and mash well, either by hand or use a food processor. In a large pot, cook ground pork and beef until the pink is out. Add ham, onion, and green peppers. Cook until the onion is clear and then add the tomatoes. Cook down until most of the liquid is absorbed. Add remaining seasonings and salt to taste. Stir in bread crumbs until desired consistency is reached. Place in a large casserole dish, top with additional Italian bread crumbs, and bake at 350 degrees for 20 minutes.

Serves 6 to 8

This basic dressing recipe is very versatile as it makes a wonderful stuffing for green bell peppers. Use very small green peppers with the tops and interior seeds removed. The stuffed peppers topped with bread crumbs can be baked in a shallow pan filled with a little water in a 350 degree oven for 25 minutes. If you don't have any mirliton or eggplant, the meat mixture does just as well without it.

Margaret H. Trahan

To this day when I see a crystal bowl, I recall it filled to the brim with sliced Creole tomatoes of brilliant red. The menu usually also included marinated cucumber slices, fresh snap beans, field peas, and stewed okra. For some reason, the meal focused around these wonderful items rather than on the meat or fish that was being served. So secondary in importance was the main entree that I have no memory whatsoever of what else we ate besides vegetables at those summer feasts!

My grandmother's real specialty, however, was her dressing which she made with either eggplant or mirliton (vegetable pear) depending on what was the most plentiful at the time. Like most children, I was very suspicious of any food that sounded the least bit exotic. Eggplant and vegetable pear worried me. How could things that looked so weird and that could not easily be bought at the A&P be any good? And yet the grown-ups raved over Gage's dressing, not bothering to even offer us kids any, they said, because we wouldn't appreciate it. They seemed to want it all for themselves.

I wonder now if Mama, Aunt Lexa, Gage and Papa were using reverse psychology on us. I somehow felt that I was finally a grown-up myself at the age of 11 when I asked for a serving of vegetable pear dressing for myself. Only then did I finally understand what all the fuss had been about.

AUNT PEG'S SCALLOPED POTATOES

1 (2 pound) package frozen hash brown potatoes
½ cup melted butter or margarine
1 teaspoon salt
1 can cream of chicken soup (undiluted)

2 cups grated sharp cheddar cheese
½ cup chopped onions
2 cups sour cream
2 cups crushed corn flakes (mixed with ¼ cup butter)

Thaw potatoes. In a mixing bowl, combine potatoes with all remaining ingredients except corn flake mixture. Put into a 9 x 13 inch baking dish. Sprinkle corn flakes on top. Bake at 350 degrees for 45 minutes.

This dish can be prepared in advance and frozen until ready to bake.

Sharon Tietbohl

CREAMY GOURMET SCALLOPED POTATOES

1 large clove minced garlic
1 chopped shallot
3 tablespoons melted butter
1¼ cups milk
1½ cups whipping cream
½ teaspoon salt

¼ teaspoon pepper
2½ pounds red potatoes, cut into ⅛ inch slices
4 ounces Gruyère cheese
¼ cup grated Parmesan cheese

Sauté first 3 ingredients for 2 minutes. Add next 4 ingredients. Mix together. Add potatoes and bring to a boil over medium heat. Transfer to 9 x 12 inch Pyrex casserole dish. Add Gruyère cheese and top with Parmesan cheese. Bake at 350 degrees for 45 minutes. Let stand 20-30 minutes before serving.

Terri Foret

GOURMET POTATOES

6 medium potatoes
2 cups shredded Velveeta
  cheese
¼ cup butter
1 ½ cups sour cream

⅓ cup chopped green onions
1 teaspoon salt
¼ teaspoon pepper
Paprika
2 tablespoons butter

Boil potatoes with skins. Cool and dice. In a heavy saucepan over low heat melt cheese and butter. As soon as melted, remove from heat and blend in sour cream, onions, salt and pepper. Fold in diced potatoes and mix gently. Pour into a greased 9 x 13 inch Pyrex dish. Dot with 2 tablespoons of butter and sprinkle paprika lightly over top. Bake at 350 degrees for 20-25 minutes.

8-10 servings

Leisa H. Comeaux

NEW POTATOES CARAWAY

1 pound new potatoes
2 tablespoons salad or olive
  oil
2 tablespoons butter
1 finely chopped clove
  garlic

3 finely chopped sprigs
  parsley
Chopped green onion
  tops
1 teaspoon caraway seeds
1 teaspoon salt
Pepper to taste

Boil potatoes with peeling until tender. Peel and cut into small cubes. Melt oil and butter in saucepan and sauté garlic. Add this to potatoes. Season with parsley, green onion tops, caraway seeds, salt and pepper. Mix thoroughly and press firmly into a well greased hot 6 or 7 inch skillet. Cook potatoes over medium heat until bottom is brown. Place in broiler to brown top. Remove from skillet and serve immediately on a hot platter.

Delicious served with pork chops.

Mary Usner

NEW POTATOES WITH HERBS

1 ½ pounds new potatoes
⅓ cup flour
½ teaspoon thyme
½ teaspoon marjoram
1 clove minced garlic

1 bay leaf
3 tablespoons margarine or
   butter
¾ teaspoon salt
Pepper to taste

Preheat oven to 450 degrees. Spray a shallow casserole dish with no stick oven spray. Scrape potatoes. Make a mixture of flour, thyme, marjoram, salt and pepper. Dip potatoes into this mixture and place in casserole dish. Add the garlic, bay leaf, and butter. Cover tightly and bake for 40 minutes or until tender when tested with a fork.

4-5 servings

Mary Usner

SWEET POTATO CASSEROLE

3 cups cooked yams
   (4 sweet potatoes)
½ cup sugar
½ cup butter

2 beaten eggs
1 teaspoon vanilla
⅓ cup milk

Topping:

⅓ cup melted butter
1 cup light brown sugar

½ cup flour
1 cup chopped pecans

Bake yams, peel and mash pulp. Mix in sugar, butter, eggs, vanilla and milk. Put into a 13 x 9 inch baking dish. For the topping, melt butter and mix in remaining ingredients. Sprinkle on top of potato mixture. Bake at 25 minutes at 350 degrees.

8-10 servings

Allison Bean

NEE'S SWEET POTATOES

1 (32 ounce) can of whole
or cut sweet potatoes
(drain but keep some of
the juice)

10 bacon strips (cut in half)
½ cup peach or orange
brandy
Ground cinnamon

Wrap each portion of potato with a half strip of bacon; secure with a toothpick. Arrange in an oven proof dish. Pour brandy over potatoes (as much as you like). Add just enough juice from potatoes to be sure potatoes do not stick. Sprinkle cinnamon generously over all potatoes. Bake in 350 degree oven until bacon cooks. May also be cooked in microwave.

Elaine Mann

EASTER SPINACH PIE

4 large eggs
2 (10 ounce) packages
chopped frozen spinach
3 tablespoons olive oil
2 finely chopped onions

1 pound cooked diced ham
1 cup ricotta cheese
1 ½ cups Parmesan cheese
Salt and pepper to taste
4 (10 inch) pastry pie shells

Preheat oven to 425 degrees. In a large bowl, beat eggs until foamy. Cook spinach according to package directions and drain. Heat olive oil in a skillet and sauté onions until wilted. Add spinach and onions to eggs in bowl. Add ham, Parmesan cheese, ricotta cheese, salt and pepper. Fill two pastry shells with filling and top with remaining two shells. Cut 6 one-inch steam vents. Seal and flute edges. Bake at 425 degrees for 40 minutes or until pie crust is golden. Cool on wire rack 10 minutes before serving.

8 servings

Barbara Guidry Bills

SENSATIONAL SPINACH PIE

1 pound Italian sausage, casing removed, cooked, crumbled
8 ounces ricotta cheese
8 ounces Mexican Velveeta shredded cheese
1 (10 ounce) package frozen spinach, thawed and drained
1 (8 ounce) herb and garlic soft cream cheese
4 ounces shredded mozzarella cheese
2 eggs, beaten
½ teaspoon hot sauce
1 package refrigerated pie crust (2 crusts)

Preheat oven to 400 degrees. Mix first six ingredients with the two eggs and hot pepper sauce until well blended. On lightly floured surface roll out pie crust to 12 inch circle and put in pie plate. Fill with sausage mixture. Roll remaining crust and put on top of pie. Brush with egg and bake 35 to 40 minutes. Serve warm or at room temperature.

Serves 10

Robin Paul Bonin

Acadiana Culinary Classic 1992 Le Petit Classique first place winner.

LEMON SQUASH

1 stick butter
1 thinly sliced lemon
6 thinly sliced yellow squash
6 thinly sliced zucchini squash
1 chopped medium onion
Salt and pepper to taste

In a large skillet, melt the butter over medium heat. Add remaining ingredients. Mix well. Cover skillet and sauté for 7-10 minutes over medium heat. Remove lemons. Serve immediately.

6-8 servings

Barbara Martin

THE BACK PORCH OF MY CHILDHOOD

I remember huge brown paper bags standing tall and upright on our back porch—filled with a variety of summer vegetables brought by friends with acres of farm land. Each bag stood there like a khaki-colored cornucopia until its contents could be cooked and prepared for the freezer. But one summer vegetable was not destined for the icy depths: the yellow summer squash. A delicious Summer Squash Casserole was cooked and served on the same day. It's a dish that brings back memories of that great array of summer vegetables spread across the back porch of my childhood home.

SUMMER SQUASH CASSEROLE

2 pounds washed and sliced yellow squash
4 tablespoons margarine
½ cup chopped onion
½ cup chopped bell pepper
½ cup grated mild cheddar cheese
½ cup mayonnaise
1 teaspoon sugar
1 egg, beaten
Fresh parsley, chopped for topping
Freshly crumbled round buttery crackers

Cook squash in boiling, salted water until tender, about 5 to 7 minutes. Drain well. Sauté onions and bell pepper in margarine until wilted. Combine with drained squash. Fold in cheese, mayonnaise, sugar, egg, salt and pepper. Pour into greased 1½ quart casserole dish. Top with parsley and crackers. Bake uncovered for 30 minutes in preheated 350 degree oven.

Suitable for freezing

Serves 8

Carol Ann Roberts Dumond

Mom's Cornbread Dressing

1 pound breakfast sausage
6 tablespoons margarine
1 cup chopped onions
2 cups chopped celery
2 tablespoons chopped parsley
2 tablespoons chopped green onions
1 cup chopped bell pepper
2 (8 ounce) packages cornbread dressing mix
¾ cup water
1 (14½ ounce) can chicken broth
Pepper to taste

Brown sausage, drain well. Sauté vegetables in margarine until wilted. Mix dressing mix with water. Combine sausage, vegetables, dressing mix and chicken broth and stir until well blended. Put mixture into a 9 x 12 inch glass pan. Cover with foil and bake at 350 degrees for 40 minutes.

8-10 servings

Jeannie Simon

Curried Fruit

1 can peaches
1 can pears
1 can pitted cherries
1 can pineapple slices
1 banana
2 tablespoons cornstarch
1 tablespoon curry powder
1 tablespoon cinnamon
1 cup brown sugar
1 stick of butter

Drain fruits and place in baking dish. Combine dry ingredients and sprinkle over top. Melt butter and pour over all. Bake 30 minutes in preheated 350 degree oven until hot and bubbly.

Serves 6

Mona Fitzgerald

MOTHER'S CORNBREAD DRESSING

1 large chicken
2 chicken bouillon cubes
1 pound pork sausage
2 tablespoons cooking oil
2 chopped bell peppers
2 chopped onions
3 chopped celery ribs
1 can cream of mushroom
   soup

5 eggs
2 teaspoons black pepper
1 ½ teaspoons garlic salt
2 teaspoons sage
6 slices of white bread,
   cubed
1 9 x 13 inch pan crumbled
   cornbread (see recipe
   below)

Place chicken in large pot, cover with water, add bouillon cubes and boil until tender. Remove from pot, reserve broth and debone chicken. Sauté sausage in large frying pan until done. Remove sausage from pan, add 2 tablespoons cooking oil and sauté onions, bell peppers, and celery until tender. In large mixing bowl mix deboned chicken, sausage, sautéed vegetables, cream of mushroom soup, eggs, seasonings, white bread and cornbread. Add chicken broth until mixture stirs easily. Pour into greased Dutch oven and bake at 300 degrees for approximately 1 ½ hours or until center of dressing is firm but not dry.

Cornbread:

4 cups self-rising cornmeal
2 eggs
⅓ cup all-purpose flour

4 tablespoons oil
2 tablespoons sugar
3 cups milk

Mix all ingredients, pour into greased 9 x 13 inch pan. Bake at 350 degrees for 45 minutes or until brown.

12-14 servings

Donna Rayburn

BIG MAMA'S CORN BREAD

I truly admired my mother-in-law. She was part of a breed of women much hardier than most of us would want to be. She endured hardships beyond what I had known, and yet managed to find love and joy in the midst of the demanding and often grueling tasks of the agricultural world she grew up in. At a young age, she fed not only a large family, but also the workers on the farm, with few things resembling the state-of-the-art kitchen equipment we have today. She couldn't reach into the fridge, pull out a can of Hungry Jacks and pop them open, but at every meal she served hot bread—cornbread or homemade biscuits. Wonderful, warm, homemade bread is special in my family today. It's delicious, and it calls up memories of a remarkable lady.

LINGUINE WITH FRESH TOMATO SAUCE

4 tablespoons olive oil
2 tablespoons minced garlic
3 pounds very ripe chopped
  tomatoes
½ cup chopped fresh basil
3 tablespoons red wine
  vinegar

Salt and freshly ground
pepper
1 pound linguine
Freshly grated Parmesan
cheese

Mix first 6 ingredients in a non-aluminum bowl. Let stand 6 hours. Just before serving, cook linguine in salted water until just tender. Drain well and cool linguine under cold tap water. Add sauce and pass the Parmesan cheese.

6 servings

Allison Bean

LINGUINE WITH PROSCIUTTO AND OLIVES

8 ounces linguine
2-3 ounces Prosciutto, cut
  into ¼ inch slices
⅛ cup olive oil
½ cup sliced green onions

3 ounce jar pimento-stuffed
  green olives, drained
1 cup halved cherry
  tomatoes
Grated Parmesan cheese

Cook linguine as package directs, drain. Meanwhile, sauté Prosciutto in hot olive oil, in a large skillet, until lightly browned. Add olives and tomatoes and cook, shaking pan often, until olives are hot, about 2 minutes. Pour Prosciutto mixture over hot noodles and toss well. Serve warm, offer cheese on the side.

4 servings

Tina Roy

OYSTER DRESSING

2 large chopped onions
6 bunches chopped green onions
1 bunch chopped parsley
6 cloves minced garlic
6 stalks chopped celery

1 ½ loaves PoBoy bread, dried out
¾ gallon oysters (reserve water)
2 large cooking spoonfuls bacon drippings
Salt and pepper

Sauté all chopped seasonings in bacon drippings until tender. Add oysters. Cook 12 to 15 minutes, stirring. In another bowl, moisten bread with oyster water, then crumble bread and add to seasoning and oyster mixture. Cook 15 more minutes. Place in large baking dish and bake at 350 degrees for 1 hour.

15 to 20 servings

If desired add chopped turkey liver to dressing before baking.

Martha Ayars

OYSTER-BREAD DRESSING

1 large loaf stale French bread
½ pound saltine crackers
1 cup milk
2 eggs, beaten
2 pounds ground pork
1 large chopped onion
½ chopped bell pepper
2 stalks chopped celery

3 minced cloves garlic
2 tablespoons flour
2 tablespoons oil
1 quart oysters, drained
2-3 tablespoons Parmesan cheese
Pimentos
Paprika

Soak crumbled bread and crackers in milk, mix well. Add eggs and stir well. Brown pork and add onion, bell pepper, celery and garlic, and cook until wilted. Make roux with flour and oil. Add to meat mixture. Add cracker mixture and mix well. Halve oysters and gently fold into mixture. Place in large, shallow baking dish. Sprinkle with Parmesan cheese and garnish with pimento and paprika. Cover with foil and bake 25 to 30 minutes at 350 degrees.

12 servings

Karen McGlasson

ESTELLE'S RICE DRESSING

5 chopped medium onions
1 chopped bell pepper
1 chopped hot pepper
1 chopped mild pepper
2 stalks chopped celery
  Roux
3 pounds ground beef
1 pound lean ground pork
1 pound finely chopped
  chicken livers

1 pound finely chopped
  chicken giblets
1 cup water
4 dozen oysters
1 quart green onion tops
3 cups cooked rice
  Salt to taste
  (Chicken livers and giblets
  can be omitted)

Add onions, peppers and celery to two large stirring spoons of roux. When wilted, add pork and ground beef. Let cook on very low heat two hours. Add liver and giblets. Cook thirty minutes. Add water (1 cup) to keep it moist and not runny. When you are ready to serve, add oysters and green onion tops. Let cook until oysters are done (about 5 minutes). Add rice to mixture.

The above mixture (without oysters) can be frozen for months.

16 servings

Estelle Barras
Gina Rush Calogero

EXTRA GOOD RICE CASSEROLE

1 stick oleo
1 medium chopped onion
½ medium chopped bell
  pepper
1 stalk chopped celery
2 cups cooked rice
1 (11½ ounce) can cream of
  celery soup (undiluted)

⅛ teaspoon garlic powder
¼ teaspoon Tony Chachere's
  seasoning or to taste
2 chopped green onions
1 tablespoon chopped
  parsley
½ cup Italian bread crumbs
1 cup grated cheddar cheese

Preheat oven to 350 degrees. Sauté onion, bell pepper, celery in oleo. Add rice, soup, garlic powder, Tony Chachere's seasoning, green onions and parsley. Mix well and adjust seasonings to your taste. In a greased 2 quart casserole dish, layer half of the rice mixture and top with ¼ cup bread crumbs and ½ cup grated cheddar cheese. Add remainder of rice mixture and top with remainder of bread crumbs and cheddar cheese. Cover and bake for 45 minutes at 350 degrees.

6 servings

Peggy Lee

RICE

1 cup long grain rice
2 cups chicken stock,
   chicken broth, or stock
   reconstituted from
   bouillon cubes
1 bay leaf

Put all three ingredients into a pot that has a tight-fitting lid. Heat on high, uncovered, until water boils. At the boiling point, reduce to the lowest heat possible, cover, and put the timer on for twenty minutes. When the time is up, if you are not ready to serve, you may remove from heat and keep covered until time to serve. The little steam holes in the surface of the rice indicate that it is cooked to perfection.

4-6 servings

Anne Simon

VRAI CADIEN

It has been said that a *Vrai Cadien*—a true Cajun— can stand at the edge of a field of rice and estimate how much gravy it would take to cover it all. It is probably the same wag who warns that, if you like your hamburger served in the traditional American style, you must tell the waitress in a Crowley, Louisiana restaurant to "hold the rice."

Both of these assertions stretch the truth a bit, but they point up the fact that, in a culinary tradition which is amazingly diverse, rice is a constant. It is impossible to imagine a Cajun meal without it. It is served in gumbo. Etouffee is served over it. Jambalaya is cooked with it. Whoever heard of eating red beans and rice without it? The list goes on and on.

Rice is not only a culinary staple, it is also a staple of the South Louisiana economy. The prairie area in the western part of Acadiana provides a perfect environment for growing rice. Crowley, Louisiana was the home of an agri-scientist who made some of history's most significant developments in rice farming. (Salmon Wright was the real life person on whom the Frances Parkinson Keyes book, Blue Camellia, was based). Crowley is recognized as "The Rice Capitol of the World."

While much of the development of rice farming in Southwest Louisiana was by settlers of German extraction, the Cajuns have been very involved. And there is this link: a popular premium beer is made with Louisiana rice.

Rice. Beer. Cajuns. A natural combination.

© FLOYD SONNIER '87
"BAYOU SUNRISE"

"BAYOU SUNRISE"

Tranquility on the bayou in the early morning has to be the most peaceful feeling one can experience. Right at sunrise when the animals are coming out of their sleep and birds are flittering about, the air is fresh and the dawn of the day is like the beginning of a time. As many mornings as possible I rise at daybreak and walk four blocks to a wooded area along Bayou Vermilion and spend a short period of my time close to nature. In these few undisturbed moments at the beginning of the day I meditate, I rejoice and I thank God for this new day. I'm sure if we could communicate with the animals and the birds, we'd hear the same.

Floyd Sonnier

ATCHAFALAYA BASIN

My old friend Steve Moore lived on the Atchafalaya levee at Bayou Benoit, near the Jolly Roger, Jr. Bar and Bourree Parlor. Steve was not a hunter. He fished. At least five days a week, you'd find him in his pirogue, fishing a barrow pit with his cane pole, number three gold hook and goose quill floater. He hauled in trophy bass. But Steve didn't mount his trophies. An accomplished artist, he would sketch his prize catch (to scale) on the cabin wall. Then we'd eat it.

The game that was cooked in Steve's kitchen came from Bayou Benoit residents, to whom the affable, erudite, loquacious blue-eyed giant (at six-feet-plus he towered over the small, wiry levee people) was their adviser and oracle. They brought it to him as they returned from the hunt, which most of them conducted with little regard for licenses, limits or seasons. They cleaned it for him at the sink adjoining his outdoor shower, trading this service for a chance to listen to Steve's fascinating dissertations on the topics of the day.

While they cleaned, Steve chopped vegetables pulled fresh from his marvelous garden, dumping them from the piece of one-by-six lumber he used for a cutting board into an ancient iron pot. I know there was garlic, shallots, seasonings he grew in the rich soil of the basin, and what else I know not. He used no recipe. He gave the game that had been taken a few hours before, a flavor that seemed to me to contain all that was rich, joyful, primitive and exciting about the great swamp.

I have eaten wild game prepared by master chefs in restaurants of renown, but none has ever matched that prepared by this remarkable man in his masterfully-built and ferociously unkept cabin deep in the Atchafalaya Basin.

MEATS AND MAIN DISHES

C'est Bon Swiss Steak

4 tablespoons canola oil
1 lean round steak - bone in
1 cup flour
1 teaspoon Tony Chachere seasoning
1 medium chopped onion
2 stalks chopped celery
½ large chopped bell pepper
2 chopped green onions

1 teaspoon garlic powder
1 (14½ ounce) can Italian stewed tomatoes, undrained
1 (6 ounce) can mushroom steak sauce and gravy
1 (6 ounce) can sliced mushrooms, drained
Salt and pepper to taste

Heat oil in heavy 4 quart pot with lid. Season steak and dredge in flour, then brown well on both sides. Remove steak to a platter and sauté onions, celery, bell pepper, and green onions in the same pot. Add garlic powder, tomatoes, steak sauce, sliced mushrooms and seasonings to taste. Cover with lid and cook at 350 degrees for 1 hour.

6 servings

Peggy Lee

Chili

1 pound ground chuck
1½ teaspoons salt
Red pepper to taste
1 clove chopped garlic
1 medium chopped onion
1 chopped celery stalk
¼ chopped bell pepper

1 (10 ounce) can whole or diced tomatoes
1 (15 ounce) can chili beans (in chili gravy)
1 tablespoon flour
3¼ tablespoons chili powder
1-2 cans of water

Season meat with salt and pepper; brown on medium heat. Add chopped vegetables and cook until softened. Add tomatoes, beans, and flour. Stir. In a cup, mix chili powder with a little water, then add to the pot. Put water in one of the bean cans and add to the pot. Stir, cover pot, and cook on medium heat for at least 1 hour, stirring occasionally. If chili is boiling, reduce heat to medium low. May need to add more water if too thick.

Susan Ducharme

CANNELLONI

Tomato Sauce:

8 tablespoons olive oil
2 cups finely chopped yellow onion
4 small cans whole tomatoes (coarsely chopped but not drained)

2 (6 ounce) cans tomato paste
1 tablespoon dried basil
4 teaspoons sugar
Salt, black pepper, red pepper to taste

Heat olive oil. Add onion, cook until soft, but not brown. Add rest of ingredients. Cook on low. Simmer for about 40 minutes or until a nice thick sauce forms.

Filling:

4 tablespoons olive oil
1 cup finely chopped onion
4 cloves minced garlic
2 (8 ounce) packages frozen spinach (chopped, defrosted, squeezed completely dry)
2 pounds ground meat
½ cup freshly grated Parmesan cheese

4 eggs, lightly beaten
1 teaspoon oregano
Salt, black pepper, red pepper to taste
2 hamburger buns made into crumbs in food processor
1 package mozzarella cheese, grated
1 package manicotti noodles

Heat olive oil, add onion and garlic. Cook until soft, but not brown. Add ground meat and cook until lightly browned, stirring to break up lumps. Add spinach and mix well. Add remaining ingredients (except mozzarella cheese) and mix thoroughly. Taste and season with salt, pepper, red pepper. Add mozzarella cheese and mix gently. This will stuff 14 manicotti noodles.

White Sauce:

6 tablespoons butter
6 tablespoons flour
1½ cups milk

2 cartons heavy cream
1½ teaspoons salt
White pepper to taste

In a heavy saucepan, melt the butter over moderate heat. Remove the pan from the heat and stir in the flour. Pour in the milk and cream, stirring constantly. Then return the pan to high heat and cook, stirring constantly. When the sauce comes to a boil reduce the heat. Simmer, still stirring until the sauce is thick. Remove the sauce from the heat, and season with salt and white pepper.

Cannelloni *(continued)*

Cook 1 package manicotti noodles in hot boiling, oiled salted water until tender. Rinse in cool water, drain in colander. Stir gently not to break. Put a film of tomato sauce at bottom of rectangular baking dish. Stuff noodles with meat mixture. Lay the cannelloni side by side in one layer on the tomato sauce. Pour white sauce over noodles. Spoon rest of tomato sauce on top. Scatter freshly grated Parmesan cheese on top. Bake cannelloni covered for about 15 minutes in a 375 degree oven. Remove foil, reduce oven to 350 degrees, continue cooking until very hot. At no time allow cannelloni to heat rapidly and boil, as your sauces will thin. This freezes well. Allow to completely defrost before baking. Does best at room temperature when put in oven.

Serves 14

Marguerite Major Smith

CORN PONE PIE

1 pound ground round	2 drops hot pepper sauce
Salt & pepper	1 teaspoon chili powder
2 tablespoons bacon grease	1 can red kidney beans
½ chopped onion	1 (16 ounce) can sliced
2 tablespoons	tomatoes
Worcestershire sauce	1 package cornbread mix

Salt and pepper meat. Put bacon grease in large frying pan. Brown chopped onion in bacon grease. Add meat and brown with onion. Drain the grease. Add Worcestershire sauce, hot pepper sauce and chili powder. Stir until well mixed. Add beans and tomatoes and simmer 10 minutes. Add water if necessary to get slightly moist mixture. Mix corn bread according to directions on package. Put meat mixture in baking dish, pour corn bread on top and bake in oven at 375 degrees until bread is golden crisp. Serve like deep dish pie.

Bob Boese

CRESCENT ITALIAN CAKE

2 pounds ground meat
1 cup chopped onion
1 teaspoon salt
1 teaspoon pepper
½ teaspoon crushed oregano
½ teaspoon basil
2 (8 ounce) cans tomato
   sauce
1 (4 ounce) can drained
   mushrooms
1 (8 ounce) carton sour
   cream
2 cans crescent dinner rolls
1 pound shredded cheddar
   cheese

Brown meat and onion. Drain. Add salt, pepper, oregano, basil, tomato sauce, sour cream and mushrooms. Spread onto crescent dinner rolls. Roll up and put in 9 x 13 inch pan and top with cheese. Bake at 350 degrees for 25 minutes.

Jason Domingue

Acadiana Culinary Classic 1992 Le Petit Classique second place winner.

MEATBALLS AND SPAGHETTI

Sauce:

3 tablespoons olive oil
½ cup chopped onion
1 clove chopped garlic
2 (20 ounce) cans of
   tomatoes
1 (8 ounce) can tomato
   sauce
1 (6 ounce) can tomato
   paste
1 cup water
1 teaspoon basil
2 tablespoons parsley
2 teaspoons salt
½ teaspoon pepper

Sauté onion and garlic in olive oil. Add canned tomatoes, tomato sauce, tomato paste, water, basil, parsley, salt and pepper. Simmer sauce over low heat about 1 hour. Stir often or it will stick.

Meatballs:

¾ pound ground meat
¼-½ pound ground pork
½ cup seasoned bread
   crumbs
½ cup Parmesan cheese
1 tablespoon parsley
1 clove minced garlic
½ cup milk
2 beaten eggs

Mix all ingredients with hands. Roll into small balls and brown on all sides. Add to sauce and continue to cook for 30 to 45 minutes.

Leslie Corey

Microwave Mexican Manicotti

½ pound lean ground beef
1 cup refried beans
1 teaspoon dried crushed oregano
½ teaspoon ground cumin
10 manicotti shells
1¼ cups water
1 (8 ounce) can picante sauce or taco sauce
1 (8 ounce) carton dairy sour cream (optional)
¼ cup finely chopped green onion
¼ cup sliced pitted ripe olives
½ cup shredded Monterey Jack cheese

Combine ground beef, refried beans, oregano and cumin; mix well. Fill uncooked manicotti shells with meat mixture. Arrange in 10 x 6 x 2 inch baking dish. Combine water and picante sauce or taco sauce; pour over manicotti shells. Cover with vented plastic wrap. Cook in microwave oven on HIGH for 10 minutes; giving dish a half-turn once. Using tongs, turn shells over. Cook covered, on MEDIUM for 17 to 19 minutes or until pasta is tender, giving dish a half-turn once. Combine sour cream, green onions and olives. Spoon down center of casserole; top with cheese. Cook uncovered, on HIGH for 2 to 3 minutes or until cheese melts.

4 servings

Nannette Kidder

No Peek Beef

1½ pounds stew meat
1 envelope onion soup mix
1 can cream of mushroom soup
1 (10 ounce) bottle club soda

Preheat oven to 325 degrees. In an 8 inch square baking dish, layer the above ingredients in order. Cover well with aluminum foil—no peeking allowed during the baking process. Bake for 2½ hours and serve over rice.

Serves 5 or 6

This dish was a staple in our college days of apartment living. Short on time, money, and cooking skills, the recipe made the toughest stew meat as tender as could be with lots of delicious gravy for rice. Now, it's an easy recipe for the kids to do.

Lillee Smith Gelinas
Clelie Dalton Sinne
Margaret H. Trahan

LAZY DAY STEW

2-2½ pounds chuck stew meat
1 package dehydrated onion
   soup mix
1 can mushroom soup

1 (8 ounce) can sliced
   mushrooms with juice
½-¾ cup of water

Mix all ingredients together and put in a 4 quart casserole dish. Cover and bake 3 hours at 325 degrees. Serve with rice or noodles.

Can also cook in a crock pot on LOW setting for 8 hours.

Kay Harper

OPIE'S LASAGNA

2 tablespoons olive oil
1 cup chopped onion
1 cup chopped celery
½ chopped green pepper
1 clove minced garlic
1½ pounds lean ground beef
1 (28 ounce) can tomatoes
2 (6 ounce) cans tomato
   paste
1 small can mushroom
   pieces
1¼ teaspoons salt

1 tablespoon sugar
1 teaspoon oregano
½ teaspoon black pepper
¼ teaspoon basil
1 bay leaf
1 package lasagna noodles
½ pound shredded
   mozzarella cheese
½ pound ricotta or cottage
   cheese
½ cup Parmesan cheese

Sauté first five ingredients for five minutes. Add ground beef and cook until browned. Put in large saucepan with remaining ingredients except cheeses and noodles and simmer for two hours, stirring occasionally. Cook noodles according to package directions and drain.

In a greased oblong baking dish, place the following layers:

3 noodles
   Sauce
   Parmesan cheese
   Mozzarella cheese
   Ricotta or cottage cheese

Repeat first layer
Noodles
Parmesan cheese
Sauce

On a cookie sheet, bake at 350 degrees for 35 minutes (or an hour if sauce is cold). When done, top of sauce will be slightly browned. Let cool 10 minutes before serving.

12 servings

Pegge Bogle

MEAT LOAF ROLL

1 (10 ounce) package
chopped broccoli
2 pounds ground chuck
1 pound ground lean pork
3 eggs
1 cup soft bread crumbs
⅓ cup catsup
⅓ cup evaporated milk
1 teaspoon salt
½ teaspoon red pepper
½ teaspoon black pepper

¼ teaspoon dried oregano
leaves
1 teaspoon Accent
⅓ cup chopped onion
⅓ cup chopped green
pepper
1 teaspoon salt
1 (3 ounce) package smoked
sliced ham
3 slices mozzarella cheese

Preheat oven to 350 degrees. Rinse frozen broccoli under cold running water to separate; drain. Mix the next thirteen ingredients thoroughly. Pat mixture into a 12 x 10 inch rectangle on a piece of wax paper. Arrange broccoli on hamburger, within ½ inch from edge. Sprinkle with 1 teaspoon salt. Arrange ham on broccoli; roll up. Place in shallow pan. Bake uncovered for 1 hour and 15 minutes. Top with cheese and bake an additional minute.

Chanda White

Acadiana Culinary Classic 1992 Le Petit Classique first place winner.

RUTH'S CHRIS STEAKS AT HOME

4 steak filets (or quality
meats)
1 stick butter

¼ cup olive oil
Salt and pepper to taste

Preheat oven to 375 degrees. Season steaks with salt and pepper to taste. Melt ½ stick of butter in black iron skillet. Add olive oil to pot when butter has melted. Sear steaks in skillet. Cook to almost desired doneness. Remove steaks from skillet and place on rack in roasting pan into oven. Place dinner plates into oven to warm. Leave steaks in oven for 7 to 10 minutes until meat has reached desired doneness. Melt other ½ of stick of butter. Pour more melted butter on steaks when taken out of oven and serve on plates. Garnish with fresh parsley sprigs. Serve with baked potatoes and sautéed fresh mushrooms.

4 servings

Lise Anne Dumond Slatten

RAVE REVIEW ROAST

1 Roast (any size). Must be a cut that is normally cooked uncovered in oven. Either boneless rump, eye round, boneless rib or standing rib, beef or pork

Nutmeg
Garlic powder (not garlic salt)
Black pepper
Ground oregano
Basil

Place roast in pan, on rack, and season so that excess seasoning stays in pan to flavor gravy. Season with nutmeg, garlic powder, black pepper, ground oregano and basil. Do not skimp on the seasonings. Season liberally and pat seasoning into meat. The nutmeg is the secret ingredient here so use plenty. It gives the meat a delicious flavor plus aids in the browning process. Never, never put salt on an uncooked roast. Salt draws the juices out of the meat and makes it dry. Place roast with the fat side up so the fat will baste roast as it cooks. If there is no fat on the roast, spray the roast with Pam cooking spray. Place seasoned roast in hottest possible oven for 20 minutes. After 20 minutes reduce oven temperature to 350 degrees and continue cooking for remainder of time. Do not open oven during first half hour of cooking.

Timing the roast: 35 minutes per pound for a beef roast. (A 3 pound roast = 1 hour 45 minutes) 45 minutes per pound for pork at 325 degrees. The first twenty minutes at 500 degrees is included and is part of the total cooking time.

Judy Corne

WINTER BRISKET

1 whole brisket
1 bottle dry white wine

1 bottle soy sauce
2 packages meat marinade

Trim brisket of most visible fat. Pour rest of the ingredients over the meat. Marinate for 2 to 3 days, turning every 24 hours. Bake at 350 degrees for 30 to 45 minutes per pound. Makes a wonderful gravy!

Erin Meyers

CIVILIZED STEAK

My father was a man of strong views and opinions. He was unyielding in his belief that a well done steak, particularly when smeared with catsup, was fit only for the uncivilized. He was determined that his children would not grow up to embarrass him by ordering, in a public place, a piece of meat cooked in such a barbaric way.

To assure that this would never happen, he sat us down every Saturday night to steaks he grilled himself, to his own taste; we were not consulted on how we wanted ours cooked. They came to us "rare," according to his description, but "red and squiggly" according to ours. I remember offering the opinion that they were subjected to so little heat that a good veterinarian could probably revive them. He was amused but not deterred. All steaks came off the grill when his was ready.

(We kids would have preferred a bowl of Cocoa Krispies. In fact, when he left the table, we dove for the box of cereal.)

But his method—harsh as it seemed to us at the time—achieved his goal. Thanks to him, I thoroughly enjoy a good steak now, cooked in a way he would have considered "civilized."

STEAK AU POIVRE

Cracked black pepper
2 **1½ inch ribeyes or filets**
¼ **cup vermouth**
1 **tablespoon lemon juice**
Dash Worcestershire sauce
4 **tablespoons cognac**
Salt
2 **tablespoons butter**
1 **tablespoon oil**
Watercress

Place 1 heaping teaspoon of cracked pepper on steaks. Pound in the pepper. Let sit at room temperature 1 hour. In a cup mix vermouth, lemon juice, Worcestershire sauce and cognac. Sprinkle salt in a heavy skillet. Heat skillet. When salt begins to brown, add butter and oil. Sear meat on both sides. Cook about 2½ minutes on each side for rare meat. Place meat on warm platter. Add the cognac mixture to the butter in the pan. Heat until bubbly. Pour over meat. Serve at once garnished with watercress. For Steak au Vers, omit black pepper. Sear meat. Add ¾-ounce green peppercorns, drained, and ⅓ cup whipping cream to sauce.

Serves 2

Margaret LaBorde

And when I watch the reaction of my children to the "red squiggly meat" I serve them every Saturday night, I experience the same sort of pleasure and satisfaction my father must have known.

CHICKEN FETTUCINE

¼ cup butter
¼ cup olive oil
1 pound cubed chicken breast
½ cup chopped green onion
2 cloves minced garlic
1 cup whipping cream
1 package Pasta Prima Alfredo Sauce
12 ounces fresh mushrooms, thinly sliced

1 (15 ounce) can stewed tomatoes, drained and diced
1 teaspoon salt
½ teaspoon black pepper
¼ cup parsley
2 tablespoons dried basil
1 pack fettucini noodles, cooked
½ cup Parmesan cheese

Heat butter and olive oil. Add chicken, green onions and garlic and sauté until chicken is lightly browned. Stir in remaining ingredients except for noodles and Parmesan cheese. Reduce heat and simmer three to five minutes. Add noodles and Parmesan cheese. Top with a little Parmesan cheese before serving.

Tressie Cox

CHICKEN FLORENTINE ROLL-UPS

1 package frozen creamed spinach, thawed
4-6 ounces grated mozzarella cheese

½ cup Italian bread crumbs
1 package boneless, skinless chicken breasts, pounded flat

In a mixing bowl, combine thawed creamed spinach, cheese and bread crumbs. More bread crumbs may be used, if needed, to keep this "stuffing" together. Season pounded chicken breasts and put spinach mixture down center of each breast. Roll up breast and place seam-side down in a Pam coated 8 x 8 inch dish. Bake at 350 degrees for approximately 45 minutes covered. Remove cover and continue baking another 15 minutes to brown the chicken breasts. Any scraps of chicken and any extra stuffing can be placed in a dish around roll ups.

Annette L. Bradley

It was a little difficult to admit early in the marriage, but now I have no problem confessing that my husband is a better cook than I am. The most striking proof is his chicken stew. It is absolutely delicious—and would make any wife jealous of her husband's superior culinary skills.

The recipe, of course, exists only in his head. Even were it written, it would be more than my simple cooking style could accommodate. Finally, he shared with me a simplified version that didn't demand his enviable expertise. Using it, I can fix a delicious supper in just an hour and a half. The family enjoys it, and I enjoy preparing it.

CHICKEN FRICASSÉE

1 large hen, cut up
4 tablespoons cooking oil
4 tablespoons flour
2 chopped onions
1 bunch chopped green onions
3 cloves chopped garlic
4 cups water
  Salt
  Black pepper
  Red pepper
4-5 sprigs chopped parsley
3 cups hot cooked rice

Heat oil in iron pot, then add cut up seasoned chicken and brown on all sides slowly. Remove chicken. On a low flame, gradually add flour to make roux, stirring constantly with wooden spoon. When mixture turns a dark mahogany color (in about 35 minutes) add 4 cups of water. Raise heat until mixture boils and add onions, green onions and garlic. Lower heat, cover, and cook for 45 minutes. Add chicken and season to taste with salt, black pepper and red pepper. Cook until chicken is done, approximately 1 hour. During the last 15 minutes add a small amount of chopped parsley and green onions. Serve over cooked rice.

8 servings

Stephanie Toups

CHICKEN JOAN

3 potatoes
2 onions
1 bell pepper
1 cup seasoned bread
crumbs

Margarine
1 cut up, skinned chicken
1 10 x 13 inch casserole
dish

Slice potatoes, sliver onions and bell pepper. Layer potatoes, 1 onion, ½ bell pepper. Sprinkle half of bread crumbs over first layer. Place chicken on top, salt and pepper, layer remaining onions and bell pepper. Sprinkle remaining bread crumbs. Put a few pats of butter on top. Cover with tin foil. Bake in 350 degree oven for 1 hour. Remove tin foil. Bake 30 more minutes.

Serves 4

Jan DiLeo Mickey
Joan DiLeo

CHICKEN PARMIGIANA

1 package boneless skinless
chicken
2 eggs slightly beaten
1 teaspoon salt
⅛ teaspoon pepper
1 cup bread crumbs
½ cup salad oil
2 cups tomato sauce

¼ teaspoon basil
⅛ teaspoon garlic powder
1 tablespoon margarine
½ cup grated Parmesan
cheese
8 ounces mozzarella cheese,
sliced and cut in triangles

Pound chicken lightly until about ¼ inch thick. Combine eggs, salt and pepper. Dip chicken into egg mixture, then crumbs. Heat oil in frying pan and brown chicken on both sides; remove to shallow baking dish. Pour excess oil from frying pan then add tomato sauce, basil and garlic powder. Heat to boiling, simmer for 10 minutes or until thickened. Stir in margarine. Pour over chicken and sprinkle with Parmesan cheese. Cover and bake at 350 degrees for 30 minutes. Uncover and place mozzarella cheese over chicken and bake until cheese melts.

Nannette Kidder

CEMETERY CLEANING AND DINNER ON THE GROUND

Some of my most delightful food memories center around a little North Louisiana church, and a great feast of home-made food spread on long tables under the trees in the church yard. For generations, people in Louisiana's "piney-woods country" have gathered for a yearly "Cemetery Cleaning and Dinner on the Ground." I remember the men of the family hard at work cleaning the graves and grounds, while the women spread roasts, salads, vegetable dishes, casseroles, fried chicken, home-made rolls, biscuits, pies, cakes and cobblers on the carefully scrubbed tables. When the call to dinner came, I always made a dash for the chicken pie.

In these times, family members are separated by geography, but we hold to the tradition. Each year, kin folk come from far and near to keep alive the ritual of our ancestors—and to share food and memories.

CHICKEN PIE

Pastry
> 2 cups sifted flour
> ⅔ cup shortening
> ½ teaspoon salt
> Cold water

Combine flour, salt and shortening. By using two knives, blend until like coarse cornmeal. Add cold water until moist enough to form a ball. Roll out ⅔ of the pastry and line an 8 x 13 inch Pyrex dish.

Filling
> 1 large chicken or 6 chicken breasts
> 1½ cans cream of mushroom soup
> 1 cup milk
> 1½ cups chicken broth
> 2 boiled eggs
> Salt and pepper

Debone chicken after boiling. Save broth. Cut chicken into pieces. Add mushroom soup, milk, broth, eggs and salt and pepper. Use more black pepper than you ordinarily would. Pour into Pyrex dish lined with pastry. Roll out the remaining pastry and cover. Flute the edges then bake at 400 degrees for 30 minutes.

Serves 6

Patsy Glover McCord

CHICKEN POT PIE

Crust:

1¾ cups flour   ½ cup oil
    Dash salt   ¼ cup milk

Mix together ingredients and roll out into 2 pie crusts.

Filling:

1 large fryer   2 cut up boiled eggs
2-3 ribs celery, ¾-inch slices   1 small can mixed
3-4 sliced green onions   vegetables
1 tablespoon chicken broth   1 small can evaporated milk
   granules   1 can chopped mushrooms
2 (10¾ ounce) cans cream
   of chicken soup

Boil chicken in seasoned water until tender. Debone, save broth. Mix chicken with vegetables, granules, soup, eggs, milk and pepper. Add broth to make desired consistency for pie. Using crust recipe, line pan. Place filling in crust. Add a top crust. Slit top crust. Cook in preheated 375 degree oven until crust is nice and brown. Serve hot.

Karen Levy

CHICKEN AND SAUSAGE JAMBALAYA

1 (2 to 3 pound) chicken   1 can Rotel tomatoes
¼ cup oil   1 can chicken broth
¾ cup chopped celery   2 cups water
¾ cup chopped onion   2 cups uncooked rice
2 cloves chopped garlic   Salt and pepper to taste
1 pound sausage, cut into
   pieces

Puree can of Rotel in blender. Set aside. Cut up chicken and season with salt and pepper. Brown chicken evenly in oil using large heavy pot. Remove chicken. Sauté celery, onion and garlic in remaining oil. Add chicken back to pot and add remaining ingredients. If necessary to render fat from sausage, using medium skillet, heat one tablespoon oil, add sausage and brown. Add enough water to cover bottom of skillet (approximately ¼ cup) and cover skillet. Allow to cook down for 10 minutes then add to other pot. Mix everything well and bake at 350 degrees for 1 to 1½ hours, covered.

Pamela Smith

CHICKEN VEGETABLE LASAGNA

3 pounds chicken
1 cup chicken stock
9 lasagna noodles
1 tablespoon oil
1 large can whole tomatoes
3 large sliced carrots
1 large sliced onion
3 sliced zucchini
3 sliced yellow squash (optional)
2½ tablespoons margarine
1 medium chopped onion

1 small chopped bell pepper
2 stalks chopped celery
3 tablespoons flour
1½ teaspoons dried basil
1½ teaspoons Italian seasonings
1½ cups 2% milk
1 cup frozen peas
Salt and pepper to taste
¾ pound grated mozzarella cheese

Season chicken and boil until cooked. Remove bones and chop meat into bite size pieces. Reserve 1 cup of chicken broth. Cook lasagna noodles according to package directions, adding 1 tablespoon oil and salt to water. Drain and rinse with cold water. Lay flat on baking sheet and cover.

Drain and slice tomatoes, discarding excess juices. Steam carrots, zucchini, onion, and squash, if used. Melt margarine, add onion, bell pepper and celery, and cook until clear. Season vegetables while they are sauteing. Add flour and stir over low heat 1 minute. Stir in dried herbs. Slowly add milk and stock. Boil 1 minute, add steamed vegetables, diced chicken and frozen peas. Mix well and cook 5 minutes more. Adjust seasonings to taste.

Spoon enough sauce from chicken mixture to cover bottom of 9 x 13 inch glass dish. Layer 3 noodles and pour ½ of chicken mixture over noodles. Top with sliced tomatoes and sprinkle ⅓ of mozzarella over all. Top with 3 more noodles. Spread remainder of chicken mixture and top with ⅓ of mozzarella over all. Top with final 3 noodles and sprinkle remainder of cheese. Cover with foil and bake at 375 degrees until bubbly, about 40 minutes. Uncover and bake additional 5 minutes or until top is golden. Let stand 5 to 10 minutes before serving.

I make this ahead of time and freeze, especially for vacation. Once it has thawed, following baking instructions—tastes like it was just made!!

Annette Bradley

STUFFED CHICKEN BREAST

12 chicken breast halves
4 teaspoons seasoned salt
1 ½ sticks margarine
1 medium chopped onion
1 medium chopped bell
  pepper
½ cup celery
1 ½ pounds chopped shrimp
3 cups fresh bread crumbs
6 tablespoons parsley
6 tablespoons green onion
  tops
½ teaspoon salt
¼ teaspoon black pepper
¼ teaspoon red pepper
½ teaspoon garlic powder
¼ cup oil
1 can cream of mushroom
  soup
2 cups chicken broth

Preheat oven to 350 degrees. Flatten chicken breast with mallet and season with seasoned salt. Sauté onion, bell pepper and celery in margarine until clear. Add shrimp; cook for five minutes. Stir in bread crumbs, parsley, green onion, salt, red pepper, black pepper and garlic powder. Cool. Stuff breast and secure with toothpicks. Brown in oil. Place in a shallow baking dish. Combine mushroom soup and broth. Pour over stuffed breasts. Bake at 350 degrees for 1 hour.

Chanda White

Acadiana Culinary Classic 1992 Le Petit Classique first place winner.

ITALIAN CHICKEN

1 pound boneless chicken
  breast cut into 1 to 2 inch
  squares
2 eggs
  Margarine
Italian bread crumbs
1 cup mushrooms
½ cup chicken broth
6-8 ounces muenster cheese

Soak chicken for 1 hour in eggs. Roll in bread crumbs. Brown in margarine. Place in single layer in casserole dish. Cover with mushrooms and chicken broth. Bake at 350 degrees for 20 minutes. Cover with thin slices of cheese and bake for another 10 minutes.

Cindy Bloch

GRETCHEN'S E-Z CHICKEN

4 chicken breasts or 1 whole
   chicken, halved
   Salt and black pepper to
   taste
1 large sliced onion
1 large sliced tomato
½ bunch chopped parsley
2 bay leaves
4 pressed cloves garlic

½ cup red wine
¼ cup water
1 chicken bouillon cube
2 tablespoons olive oil
2 tablespoons
   Worcestershire sauce
Juice of 1 lemon
Paprika

Salt and pepper chicken on both sides. Place in Pyrex baking dish and layer onion, tomato, parsley and bay leaves on top of chicken. In a cup, mix wine and water with chicken bouillon. Cover with foil and bake for 40 minutes in 325 degree oven. Remove foil and raise oven temperature to 400 degrees and brown chicken for about 3 minutes, or until desired color is achieved. May thicken sauce with cornstarch if desired.

Serves 4

Becky Berthelot

HEN SAUCE PIQUANTE

1 hen
¼ cup steak seasoning
4 cups chopped onion
2 cups chopped bell pepper
⅓ cup minced garlic
4 bay leaves
1 teaspoon thyme
1 teaspoon rosemary

6 (12 ounce) cans chicken
   broth
1 cup roux
1 (12 ounce) can tomatoes
1 (10 ounce) can cream of
   mushroom soup
Water
2 cups chopped green onion
   Salt and pepper to taste

Cut hen into small pieces. Sprinkle with steak seasoning and brown completely in large pot. Remove hen. Leave drippings and add onions and bell pepper, garlic, bay leaves, thyme and rosemary. Sauté until tender. Add chicken broth and bring to boil. Add roux and stir constantly. Add tomatoes and can of cream of mushroom soup. Add water and stir well. Allow to cook in oven at 325 degrees for three hours. Remove and add green onions and let sit for ten minutes. Serve over rice.

Christy Weatherford

Acadiana Culinary Classic 1992 Le Petit Classique second place winner.

MARINA'S SWEDISH CHICKEN

1 chicken, cut into pieces
Salt and pepper to taste
2-3 tablespoons vegetable oil
1 large onion, quartered
1 large can mushrooms with liquid

1 large jar pimento with juice
1 bunch chopped parsley
½ cup dry sherry

Salt and pepper chicken pieces. Heat a 2-quart pot and add oil. When oil is hot, add chicken pieces and brown on both sides. Add all remaining ingredients in order listed. Lower heat, cover and cook 30 to 35 minutes.

Serves 4

Gretchen Allen

WHITE CHICKEN SPAGHETTI

6 deboned chicken breast halves
2 cups white wine
3 cups water
1 stick butter
1 large chopped onion
1 chopped bell pepper

4 stalks chopped celery
1 large can mushroom pieces, drained
3 cups shredded cheddar cheese
1 pound spaghetti
Season to taste

Boil chicken in wine and water until cooked. Remove chicken and cut into bite size pieces. Boil the package of spaghetti in the remaining liquid until the liquid cooks out. In skillet sauté onion, bell pepper, celery and mushrooms in the butter. Mix in chicken, spaghetti and cheese. Season to taste.

Lisa Breaux

BAKED HAM WITH SAUCE

1 medium ham with bone in
5 ounces cola
  (approximately)
1 teaspoon wine vinegar

1 teaspoon dry mustard
2 cups packed brown sugar
Heavy juice from medium
  can of pear halves

Core ham and remove excess fat. Put in uncovered shallow roast pan. Pour the cola over the ham and bake at 325 degrees for 1 hour. Skim off excess fat. Mix rest of ingredients and baste over ham. Cook for another 2 hours basting with sauce every 30 minutes. The sauce will thicken and you can serve it in a gravy boat along with the ham.

Marianne Schneider

SPEEDY SOUTHWEST SPAGHETTI PIE

8 ounces spaghetti
½ cup milk
1 egg
1 pound ground pork
1 medium chopped onion
1 medium chopped green
  pepper
1 large minced garlic clove
1 tablespoon chili powder
½ teaspoon ground cumin

½ teaspoon dried oregano
½ teaspoon salt
¼ teaspoon black pepper
1 (16 ounce) can tomato
  sauce
4 ounces grated Monterey
  Jack cheese with jalapeños
4 ounces grated cheddar
  cheese

Preheat oven to 425 degrees. Cook spaghetti according to package directions and drain. Whisk milk and egg together and mix with hot spaghetti. Spread mixture in buttered 9 x 13 inch pan. Cook pork, onion, bell pepper and garlic together. Add chili powder, cumin, oregano, salt and pepper. Stir in tomato sauce. Spread meat mixture over spaghetti. Sprinkle cheeses over top and bake at 325 degrees for 20 minutes.

Casey Lee Doiron

Acadiana Culinary Classic 1992 Le Petit Classique second place winner.

In Southwest Louisiana, a Cochon de Lait is more than a culinary delight, it is an occasion. Imagine a gathering of friends and family on a crisp fall day, with the warm camaraderie centered around a plump, succulent young pig turning above an open fire, roasting very, very slowly, the juices dripping into the flames and exploding into a tantalizing aroma that fills the Autumn air. Beautiful memories of my youth and of my father come flooding back when I recall that scene and that wonderful aroma.

The Cochon de Lait was my father's specialty, and he always prepared it when there was a large gathering at our house. Translated "Milk Pig," the Cochon de Lait was always the delight of guests from out-of-town, most of whom had never experienced such an occasion or such a taste treat.

On the day of a Cochon de Lait, sunrise found the fire blazing in the open pit, and the pig already turning, almost imperceptibly, on the spit. It is a lengthy process, but a wonderful occasion for being outdoors and sharing good feelings and good conversation. The mechanics of Cochon de Lait are traditionally reserved for the men of the family, and there was always an obvious delight as they gathered for the occasion.

Dad's Cochon de Lait also sent a message. When a fiancé was brought home to meet the family, Dad began shopping immediately for just the right pig.

COCHON DE LAIT

Whole suckling pig
(approximately 25 pounds)
Salt, pepper, lemon, and garlic

Allowing 1 pound of raw meat, dressed, per person, select Cochon de Lait (milk fed pig is the literal translation) according to the number of guests to be served. Season generously with basting sauce and hang on a sheet of welded mesh fencing wire folded over to encase the pig. Secure ends and hang shoulders down in front of an open pit with metal backing for heat retention. Rotate constantly, either by hand or with mechanical device and keep fire very hot and burning well. After about three hours, halfway through cooking time, reverse pig and hang with shoulders up. Cook until grease no longer drips or about 6 hours. To crisp up skin and cause it to crackle, hold pig directly over flame for 30 to 45 seconds at the end of cooking. The crackled skin is then served as an appetizer.

Martha Moreau Latiolais

The soon-to-be son-in-law was introduced to the Cochon de Lait tradition, and given the message loud and clear that the men in our family were supposed to cook!

One step remained after the roasting was complete. The pig was held directly over the flames so that the skin would crackle. The crackled skin, lifted away from the body and broken into serving pieces is known as "couenne" and is served as an appetizer while the carving of the pig takes place.

There is a tradition to the Cochon de Lait which demands certain trimmings, usually rice dressing, vegetables, salad and bread. It is a wonderful meal, a wonderful occasion, and one of my happiest food memories.

EASY PORK CHOP, RICE AND MUSHROOM CASSEROLE

4 pork chops	1 can beef consommé
4 tablespoons oil	1 cup water
2 cloves chopped garlic	1 cup uncooked rice
1 medium chopped onion	1 (8 ounce) can mushrooms
⅓ cup chopped green onions	Salt and pepper to taste
⅓ cup chopped bell pepper	

In large skillet or Dutch oven brown pork chops in 2 tablespoons oil and remove. Sauté garlic, onions and bell pepper in remaining oil. Add consommé, water, rice and mushrooms. Salt and pepper to taste, stir. Place pork chops on the top of rice. Bake at 300 degrees covered for about 1 hour or until rice is done.

Serves 4

Dee Anne Jewell

SAUSAGE AND TASSO JAMBALAYA

1 pound pork tasso	4 cups water
1 pound pork sausage	2 cups raw rice
¼ cup oil	4 teaspoons salt
½ cup diced onion	2 teaspoons black pepper
½ cup diced celery	¼ cup chopped onion tops
¼ cup diced green bell pepper	¼ cup chopped parsley

Parboil pork tasso about 15 minutes and then cut into small pieces along with sausage. Put into pot with oil and let cook for a few minutes or until brown. Add onions, celery, bell pepper and stir until clear. Next add two cups of water, stir, cover and let it come to a boil. When it begins to boil add two cups raw rice and two cups of water, salt and pepper. Stir, cover and let it return to a boil. Add onion tops and parsley, stir gently. Cover, lower temperature and cook for about 45 minutes.

Serves 12

Tina Guillory

Note: Acadiana Culinary Classic 1992 Le Petit Classique first place winner.

POT ROASTED DOVE À LA POOPSIE

6-8 doves	1 small jar sliced mushrooms
Salt	1 chicken bouillon cube
Red and black pepper	½ cup red wine
½ medium chopped onion	1 tablespoon cornstarch
3 pods minced garlic	2 cups water

Clean and wash doves. Season with salt and pepper. Place doves, breast up, in baking pot or roaster uncovered in preheated oven at 375 degrees for about 45 minutes to 1 hour or until brown. Remove from oven adding onions, garlic, mushrooms, red wine and one cup of water. Turn doves breast down, cover and return to oven for 1 to 1½ hours. Check every 30 minutes, adding water if needed. Remove doves from gravy when done. Place on top of stove on medium heat and add bouillon cube and 1 cup of water. Mix cornstarch to one tablespoon water and add to gravy to thicken. Taste for seasoning.

Serves 3 to 4

Connie Galloway

MOM'S OLD WOOD STOVE

Hot, puffy corn bread in a cast iron skillet—round steak cooking until almost black, with a gravy that brings back delicious memories of real Cajun cooking to a purist like me—coffee, black and strong, dripped with unhurried patience, the pot in a shallow pan of water to keep the coffee hot without boiling; all on my Mom's wood stove.

WILD DUCKS

Assorted wild ducks
Salt and pepper
Apples, celery and onion, chopped in chunks
Flour
Few tablespoons oil
1 cup red wine
Chicken stock or water
Chives, green onions or parsley, chopped

Remove wings, necks and pin-feathers. Rub ducks with salt and pepper. Stuff cavities with apples, celery and onions. Flour ducks lightly. Pour enough oil to cover the bottom of a heavy pot or Dutch oven and heat on high. Sear ducks to brown them and turn. Add wine and enough water or stock to cover the ducks half way. Sprinkle a little flour on top of ducks. Cover. Reduce heat so that the pot will simmer lightly, or place the pot in a 350 degree oven. Remove young ducks when meat is falling off the bone (several hours). Continue to cook larger ones. When done, remove skin and back bones. Garnish before serving.

Anne Simon

The stove, rather large and black and made from cast-iron, was the center of activity in the small kitchen. It served many purposes. The main purpose was, of course, the cooking of food for our family. The second and almost as important use of this "appliance" was to keep the kitchen warm during the cold winter months. However, during the hot summer months, Mom had to not only endure the heat of the season but also the heat of the stove. We had no electricity; so therefore, we had no air conditioning and no fans. I guess we took it in stride because I really don't remember the heat.

I remember well my Mom stirring the hot pots; holding the handles with the bottom of her apron; reaching behind the stove where the wood box was and adding another piece of wood to keep the fire hot. She would probably have pots on all four openings on top of the stove. I remember well the rice steaming; the spicy, dark (rusty) gravy from the natural juices of an over-cooked steak or roast; fresh butter-beans simmering away; smothered Irish potatoes with its "gratin" stuck to the bottom of the pot which my brother, Mervin and I would fight over; and of course, the fluffy corn bread baking in the oven. I get really hungry every time I think about it.

The kitchen was always everyone's favorite gathering place. Mom's old wood stove probably had a lot to do with that.

I would not want to go back to those days, but I treasure the memories. Sometimes I close my eyes and go back.

Floyd Sonnier

CRAWFISHING FOR FUN

A favorite past-time of ours in the Spring was to go crawfishing. All of us who lived on the farm had a pond in the back pasture, known to Cajuns as a "vivier" or "marais". Many of us also lived along or near "the woods" where there were many bayous and coulées. The crawfish in the Spring were plentiful. Of course, commercial crawfishing was unknown. You could not buy crawfish. My mother would cut pieces of fat meat or bacon and tie each piece with short strings to sticks. Early in the morning was a great time to go crawfishing. I remember it was so much fun that we would literally spend the whole day out in the woods. Our catch was then boiled. Mom would give us a few boiled ones to eat. With the rest she would make a gumbo or fricassée. Mom knew how to please us.

Floyd Sonnier

WHICH IS WHICH?

Residents of Cajun Country are often asked to explain the difference between the various culinary delights, such as etouffee, fricassée, bisque, stew, sauce piquante and crawfish gumbo. It's not easy to explain. We went to well-known Cajun author, Mary Alice Fontenot to ask her help with this, and she offered this expert dissertation, narrowing the field by using crawfish as the central ingredient of each dish. Mrs. Fontenot is the author of the delightful series of children's books based on the life and times of Clovis Crawfish.

"There is little difference—perhaps none at all—between six commonly known recipes of crawfish etouffee, crawfish fricassée, crawfish bisque, crawfish stew, crawfish sauce piquante and crawfish gumbo.

All have a common ingredient: crawfish. (They can be made with any number of ingredients: shrimp, oysters, turtle, etc., of course, but for purpose of explanation, let's stay with crawfish.) All call for some form of cooking fat (usually real butter), and all need lots of chopped onions.

If there's no roux in a crawfish gravy, it's etouffee. Etouffee means "smother," so what's done is one smothers a bunch of chopped onions in butter, adds crawfish tails and seasoning, lets it smother down a few minutes, then serves it over hot rice.

If it's a thick roux gravy, it's crawfish stew. If it's a soupy crawfish gravy and needs to be eaten with a spoon, it's crawfish gumbo.

If it's a heavy and spicy tomato gravy, it's sauce piquante.

If the crawfish tails are ground up and stuffed into the crawfish shells, it's a bisque.

Crawfish fricassée is any combination of crawfish and Louisiana vegetables for which one has no other name. If one doesn't know what it is, call it a fricassée."

FISH AND SEAFOOD

ALLIGATOR PROVENÇALE

1 chopped onion	3 cups canned tomatoes
1 small chopped green pepper	1 cup plain barbecue sauce
2 chopped ribs celery	2 pounds alligator fillets, cut into 1-inch cubes
½ stick butter	(available at seafood
2 tablespoons flour	stores)

In a large skillet, sauté the first 3 ingredients in the butter until soft. Add the flour and cook to a thick paste. Add the next 2 ingredients and simmer, covered, for 30 minutes. Add alligator and continue cooking for 1 hour or until meat is tender. Serve over rice. This recipe can be doubled.

6-8 servings

Allison Staton

CRABMEAT CASSEROLE

3 cups lump crabmeat	2 tablespoons flour
¼ pound oleo or butter	4 tablespoons grated Parmesan cheese
⅓ cup minced onion tops	2 cups water
1 tablespoon minced garlic	¼ cup bread crumbs
1 large whole bay leaf	Salt and pepper to taste
1 tablespoon parsley	

In large pot melt oleo or butter. Add flour, mix until smooth, add onion tops and garlic until tender. Add water, bay leaf, parsley, salt and pepper. Boil slowly until sauce is thickened. Fold crabmeat in carefully, cook slowly turning crabmeat in sauce, trying not to break up large lumps, about 10 minutes. Put in casserole, sprinkle the top with bread crumbs and a dash of Parmesan cheese. Bake in oven until bread crumbs are brown or sides are bubbly.

Serves 6

Charlotte Peck

BOILED CRAWFISH

1 box salt	30 pounds live crawfish
½ cup cayenne pepper	(preferably washed, the
3 ounces crab boil	cleaner the crawfish the
Vegetable oil	better)
Lemons	Onions
3 cups chopped jalapeños	Potatoes
½ cup jalapeño juice	Corn
Tony Chachere's	20 gallon boiling pot with
seasoning mixture	basket

To wash crawfish, empty sack in #3 wash tub and fill with water and let soak. Fill boiling pot ⅓ full with water. Let water heat up to near boil. Add 1 box salt, 3 ounces crab boil, ½ cup cayenne pepper, ½ cup jalapeño juice, and ⅓ cup vegetable oil. Place lid back on top of pot and let come to full boil. Fill empty basket with washed crawfish and place in pot of boiling water. Replace the lid back on top and watch for full (heavy) steam coming out the top side of pot and lid. After seeing steam, time for 3 minutes. Pull basket out of water, and let water drain, then empty into ice chest. Season with Tony Chachere according to desired hotness and add 3 cups of chopped jalapeños (better to buy the gallon jar, cheaper). Mix with crawfish using rubber gloves or heavy spoon. Cover ice chest and let sit 10 minutes or so. Add potatoes and onions to boiling water and cook 10 minutes after steam, then add corn for an additional 10 minutes.

Kevin McKay

CRAWFISH ETOUFFEE

½ cup margarine	1 minced clove garlic
1 ½ cups finely chopped	2 tablespoons flour
onions	1 pound crawfish tails
½ cup finely chopped bell	½ teaspoon salt
pepper	⅛ teaspoon red pepper

Melt margarine in skillet on medium heat; add onions, bell pepper, and garlic. Sauté until softened, about 10-15 minutes. Stir in flour. Cover and cook 10 minutes, stirring occasionally. Add crawfish tails, stir, cover, and cook on medium low for 5 minutes (until juice is produced). Add seasonings and ½ cup water, stir and let simmer. Serve over rice.

To increase amount of gravy, use 3 or 4 tablespoons of flour instead of just 2 and add enough water to produce desired consistency.

Serves 4 to 6

Susan Ducharme

ADAM'S CRAWFISH ETOUFFEE

2 sticks butter
¾ cup diced onion
½ cup diced celery
⅓ cup diced bell pepper
⅓ cup diced onion bottoms
¼ cup chopped parsley
3 tablespoons chicken bouillon
1 tablespoon paprika
1 teaspoon cayenne pepper
½ teaspoon garlic powder
½ teaspoon black pepper
1 quart water
⅛ cup flour
⅛ cup butter
3 pounds crawfish tails
2 tablespoons parsley
2 tablespoons green onion

In an 8 quart sauce pot over medium heat, melt butter and add onion, bell pepper, celery, onion bottoms and parsley. Cook until tender. Add chicken bouillon, paprika, cayenne pepper, garlic powder and black pepper. Cook and stir two more minutes. Add water and bring to a boil for 10 minutes and thicken with roux made from flour and butter. Add crawfish tails. Just before serving add parsley and green onion tops. Serve over rice.

Adam Graham

Acadiana Culinary Classic 1992 Le Petit Classique first place winner.

LISA'S CRAWFISH BROCCOLI CASSEROLE

1 pound crawfish
1 can cream of golden mushroom soup
1 large bag of chopped broccoli
1 can Rotel tomatoes
1 small package Velveeta cheese
1 stick butter
1 chopped large onion
1 chopped bell pepper (optional)
2 chopped stalks celery (optional)
1½-2 cups cooked rice
Bread crumbs
Season to taste

Sauté onions, bell pepper, and celery in butter until transparent. Add crawfish, and sauté 15 minutes. Add cooked broccoli, Rotel tomatoes, soup, cheese, and cooked rice. Mix well. Season to taste. Put in casserole dish and top with dry bread crumbs. Heat in oven or microwave until hot and bubbly.

Serves 8 to 10

Lisa Breaux

CAJUN BABIES

Cajun Baby Filling:

- 1 stick butter
- 1 cup chopped onions
- ½ cup chopped celery
- ½ cup chopped bell pepper
- 1 dozen chopped fresh mushrooms
- 3 tablespoons all-purpose flour
- ½ pound crawfish
- ¼ pound shrimp
- 1 pint whipping cream
- 1 pound processed cheese with jalapeños
- 1 pound lump crabmeat
- ¼ cup chopped green onion
- ¼ cup chopped parsley
- 1 teaspoon salt
- ½ teaspoon cayenne
- ½ teaspoon black pepper
- ½ teaspoon garlic powder
- 1 cup cooked wild rice

Sauté onions, celery, bell pepper and mushrooms in butter and cook until wilted. Add flour, continue cooking for 10 minutes. Add crawfish and shrimp and cook for seven minutes stirring occasionally. Blend in whipping cream and cheese. When cheese melts, add lump crabmeat, green onions, parsley and seasonings. Remove from heat and add wild rice.

Cajun Baby Bread for stuffing:

- 2½ cups all-purpose flour
- 2½ cups whole milk
- 7 eggs
- 5 tablespoons hot melted butter

Whisk flour, milk, eggs and butter until smooth. Pour this mixture divided evenly into ten (8 ounce) soufflé dishes. Bake for 30 minutes or until golden brown. Cut circular hole and spoon filling into each Cajun Baby Bread.

Sky Salter

Acadiana Culinary Classic 1992 Le Petit Classique first place winner.

CRAWFISH FETTUCINE

1 ½ cups butter
3 chopped onions
2 chopped small bell
   peppers
1 ¼ cups flour
4 tablespoons parsley
3 pounds crawfish tails
1 pint half and half cream
1 pound Velveeta cheese

2 teaspoons chopped
   jalapeños
2 minced cloves garlic
   Salt, red & black pepper
   or Tony Chachere's
   seasoning
1 pound cooked angel hair
   noodles
   Parmesan cheese

Sauté onions and bell pepper in butter until clear. Add flour, cover and cook 15 minutes stirring frequently. Add parsley and crawfish tails, cook covered 15 minutes, add cream, Velveeta cheese, jalapeños, garlic, salt and pepper. Cook covered 30 minutes, stir to prevent sticking. Add cooked noodles and mix thoroughly. Sprinkle Parmesan cheese on top. Bake at 350 degrees for 15 to 20 minutes.

Kathleen V. Rudick

CRAWFISH FETTUCINE MADE EASY

1 stick butter
1 cup chopped yellow onion
4 minced cloves garlic
½ cup chopped celery
1 pound crawfish tails
1 (10 ounce) can cream of
   mushroom soup
1 (8 ounce) carton sour
   cream

8 ounces of Velveeta cheese
   Cajun seasoning to taste
1 teaspoon salt
1 (8 ounce) package
   fettucine, boiled and
   drained
   Grated Parmesan cheese

Melt butter in large pot and sauté onions, celery and garlic for five minutes or until tender. Add crawfish, soup, sour cream, Velveeta cheese and seasonings. Simmer until bubbly. Add cooked noodles. Mix well and pour into a 2 quart casserole. Top with grated Parmesan cheese and bake uncovered at 350 degrees until heated through, about 25 minutes.

6 servings

Doubles easily and freezes well.

Cammie Dale

ED ROY'S CRAWFISH CASSEROLE

I believe that, at some point very close to the time of my birth, my mother was frightened by a yo-yo. My weight has followed the up and down pattern of that toy all my life. Weight loss diets are part of my early childhood memories. Eventually, however, in the midst of the feeling of deprivation that comes from limiting calories while living in the Mecca for Gourmets that is South Louisiana's Cajun Country, I discovered the recipe for Crawfish Casserole. Wonder of wonders—here was something that satisfied my love for Cajun seafood dishes—and my need to keep the calories under control. Crawfish, the staple of Cajun cooking, and vegetables. What a sneaky way to eat healthy.

CRAWFISH CASSEROLE

4 (1 pound) frozen bags yellow summer squash
1 (1 pound) frozen bag bell peppers
3 eggs
1 (1 pound) frozen bag chopped onions
24 ounces crawfish tails
8 crushed Wasa Crisps (find these in diet section of store)
1 dash butter salt
1 dash red pepper
1 dash Tony Chachere's Seasoning
1 dash chopped parsley
1 dash paprika
1 dash seafood herbs

Cook squash, onions and bell pepper down to a soft consistency; drain off excess liquid. Add crawfish and cook a few minutes more. Season with herbs. Mix egg and Wasa together and fold into mixture. Pour into 9" x 13" greased pan. Bake at 350 degrees for 30 minutes.

8 servings

Be sure to use frozen bags of vegetables as the moisture content from the vegetables is very important to the casserole.

Ed Roy

CRAWFISH PASTA SALAD

2 pounds crawfish tails
½ teaspoon liquid crab boil
2 teaspoons Tony Chachere's seasoning
2 cups water
1 (12 ounce) package small shell macaroni
½ cup Italian style dressing
½ cup chopped sweet onion
1 cup chopped celery
1 cup raw zucchini

2 tablespoons sweet pickle relish
2 tablespoons dill pickle relish
1 ⅓ cups mayonnaise
⅓ cup ketchup
2 teaspoons prepared horseradish
Salt and black pepper to taste

Place water, crab boil, and Tony's seasoning in the lower part of a steamer or rice cooker. Place crawfish tails in top part of steamer and cover. Bring water to boil, lower to medium and steam crawfish for about 15 minutes. Drain crawfish, reserving the liquid and place crawfish in refrigerator to cool.

Pour crawfish liquid into bottom of steamer and add enough water to make 6 cups. Cook shell macaroni according to package directions, drain, and place in a large mixing bowl. Toss shell macaroni in the Italian dressing. Add chopped onion, celery, zucchini, and pickle relish. Stir in cooled crawfish tails.

Mix mayonnaise, ketchup, and horseradish and stir into salad. Season with salt and black pepper to taste. Serve chilled, on lettuce leaves with soft Italian bread sticks.

This is a recipe I dreamed up to serve at a real estate open house luncheon. Everyone seemed to enjoy it so I thought I would share it with anyone who needs a simple recipe for summertime with many of the great ingredients of South Louisiana. This salad can be just as good made with shrimp. However, be sure to use the broth from steaming the shrimp to boil the pasta, as this adds to the flavor of the salad.

Serves 12 to 14

Bettye Walker

CATFISH SAUTÉ

4 fillets of catfish
1 stick butter
Salt and pepper (or Tony
Chachere seasoning)

1 chopped large onion
1 chopped small bell pepper
3 crushed pods garlic

Season catfish. Sauté in butter. Turn once and add vegetables to top of the catfish. Cover and cook until fish is done.

4 servings

Kathleen V. Rudick

———————————

BAKED FISH WITH STUFFING

3-4 orange roughy or red
snapper fillets
Salt and pepper to taste
(red or black)
1 stick margarine
1 cup French bread crumbs
(old bread, grated)
1 cup shrimp (cooked or
raw)

¼ cup milk
1 cup crabmeat (can be
imitation crab)
1 tablespoon chopped
parsley
2 tablespoons lemon juice
Tony Chachere's to taste

Select a fish suitable for baking. Sprinkle all sides of fillets with salt, pepper, lemon juice and Tony Chachere's. Lay fillets on an ungreased casserole dish. Mix bread crumbs, shrimp, crabmeat, parsley and milk (enough to moisten stuffing). Spread stuffing on fillets. Cut pats of butter and place on top of stuffing. Bake uncovered about 45 minutes at 350 degrees or until done. Serve with lemon slices.

4-8 depending on size of fish and if fillets are cut in half

Nannette (Nan) Kidder

One Saturday afternoon, we received a call from some old friends from Up North, who announced they were dropping in on us that night and were really hungry for Cajun seafood. A quick forage through our kitchen produced some catfish fillets and some crawfish tails. My thought was that the more fattening a dish is, the better I like it. So we combined all the ingredients and came up with Stuffed Catfish Fillets. Leave it to a Cajun to turn an otherwise low calorie dish into a meal that will get you offers to be the Weight Watchers poster child.

Our friends departed two pounds heavier but wouldn't leave until we gave them the recipe.

STUFFED BAKED CATFISH

2 pounds catfish fillets
1 pound crawfish
1 stick butter
1 cup chopped green onion
1-2 (8 ounce) packages cream cheese
Tabasco
Salt, pepper, parsley, onion tops to taste

Season to taste and bake catfish uncovered on a Pam coated layer of foil until golden brown in a 500 degree oven. In a separate pan, melt butter and sauté whole crawfish and green onions for about 10 minutes. Melt cream cheese into crawfish mixture and cook until bubbly. Add other seasonings. Pour on top of each fillet.

4 servings

Ed Roy

GRILLED FISH WITH SEAFOOD FETTUCINE

Fettucine Sauce:

¼ cup margarine

2 tablespoons all purpose flour

5 ounces evaporated milk

1 pound shrimp or crabmeat

1 teaspoon salt

½ teaspoon red pepper

¼ teaspoon paprika

12 ounces fettucine

2 tablespoons margarine

Fettucine Sauce: Melt margarine in a thick skillet over medium-low heat. Add the milk and flour. With a metal whisk stir constantly until smooth and creamy. Reduce heat and simmer until sauce thickens, whisking constantly. Add seafood and seasoning and cook for 10 minutes over low heat. If margarine starts to separate from the sauce, add about 1 tablespoon additional milk and continue whisking. Boil dry noodles according to package directions and drain. Return to pot and add 2 tablespoons margarine.

Fish:

1 pound fresh fish fillets

1 teaspoon salt

1 teaspoon lemon pepper

1 teaspoon Creole seasoning

¼ cup margarine

2 tablespoons minced garlic

Fish: Season fish with salt, lemon pepper and Creole seasoning. In small bowl melt margarine in microwave and add garlic to make basting sauce. Spray wire fish basket with no stick cooking spray (or spray the grill directly if not using basket). Place fish on grill and baste with garlic butter sauce. Cook 5 minutes (for medium thickness fillets) and turn. Baste and cook for 5 more minutes. Serve buttered fettucine on each plate. Top with seafood sauce. Serve fish immediately from grill.

Patrice Williams

GARFISH PATTIES

5 pounds garfish	½ cup chopped parsley
4 large potatoes	4 eggs
1 large chopped onion	Salt and pepper to taste
1 large chopped bell pepper	Flour
1 cup chopped celery	Oil

Scrape garfish off of bone. Boil potatoes and mash them. Add potatoes, onion, bell pepper, celery, parsley and eggs into the garfish and mix together. Add salt and pepper to taste. Form into patties and coat with flour. Fry in oil until golden brown. Drain on paper towel.

Serves 10

April Rene Benoit

Acadiana Culinary Classic 1992 Le Petit Classique third place winner.

BARBECUED REDFISH

½ cup butter (1 stick)	Lime juice to taste
5 ounces Worcestershire sauce	Ketchup to thicken
2 ounces Pickapeppa sauce	1 large redfish fillet with skin
3 tablespoons Tabasco sauce	

Combine first 6 ingredients in a 1 quart saucepan. Bring to simmer and cook 10-15 minutes. Brush on both the skin and meat sides of the fish. Grill fish over hot coals for approximately 10-15 minutes, beginning with meat side down. After turning the skin side down, baste with additional sauce.

Suzanne Odom & Tolley Odom

RED FISH COURT-BOUILLON

First Step -Roux:

⅔ cup flour   ½ cup oil

Blend. Place in a microwave-safe container. Microwave on high 6 minutes. Then in 30 second intervals until you reach the desired color. Transfer to large roasting pot. Heat on high and continue to brown if not yet desired color.

Second Step:

2 large onions   2-3 garlic pods
1 whole bell pepper   Hot water
3-4 celery sticks

Add vegetables to the roux and cook until onions are wilted and clear. Add hot water, mixing well, until you have about 1-1½ inches of water in bottom of pot. Cook 10-15 minutes.

Third Step:

1 can diced Rotel tomatoes   1 lemon, cut into slices,
1 small can tomato sauce   squeeze juice into pot and
1 small can tomato paste   add slices
½ teaspoon sugar

Add to above and cook for 1 or 2 hours to blend seasonings.

Fourth Step -Red Fish:

Season red fish well with salt, red/black pepper, garlic powder. I keep fish whole and score each side, then rub seasoning well into fish and scores. Add fish to Court-Bouillon and cook 15-20 minutes. (Time varies according to size of fish.) Serve in a bowl with rice. Eat with a spoon and enjoy.

You want fish to be firm and flaky, not mushy just before adding to Court-Bouillon for cooking.

Annette L. Bradley

SAC-A-LAIT SURPRISE

6 quarts water
Liquid crab boil
1 ½ pounds sac-a-lait filets
3 slices stale bread
1 small can evaporated milk
¾ stick margarine
1 large chopped onion
1 chopped bell pepper

1 chopped stalk celery
1 teaspoon minced parsley
1 can cream of mushroom
soup
Tony Chachere's Creole
seasoning
⅓ cup seasoned bread
crumbs

Bring water to boil, add liquid crab boil seasoning. Put filets in water and boil only until the filets turn white (about 7 to 10 minutes) and remove. Soak bread in milk. Melt margarine in large skillet, add onion, bell pepper, celery and parsley and sauté. Flake fish with fork and add to seasonings. Blend. Squeeze bread and tear apart and add to fish mixture. Add cream of mushroom soup and mix well. Season to taste. Pour into lightly greased 9 x 13 inch casserole dish and sprinkle with bread crumbs. Bake at 350 degrees for 25 minutes.

Serves 10

Misty Lynn Sonnier

Acadiana Culinary Classic 1992 Le Petit Classique second place winner.

LOUIS' SPECKLED TROUT

8 medium size speckled
trout fillets (other fish
may be substituted: bass,
orange roughy, catfish)
1 stick butter or margarine
4 oranges - peeled,
membrane removed, pulp
cut in half inch pieces

4 lemons - prepared like
oranges
2 cups flour
Salt, red and black pepper
to taste

Pat fillets dry, season with salt, red pepper and black pepper to taste. Place flour in plastic bag or bowl and dredge fillets to coat thoroughly. Melt butter in skillet until very hot being careful not to burn. Fry fillets until golden brown, crispy on the outside, firm on the inside. Arrange fillets on plates to serve - 2 to a plate - keep warm. Place orange and lemon bits in skillet with remaining butter on reduced heat. Cook until hot throughout, about 5 minutes. Pour orange and lemon sauce over fillets.

Serves 4

Louis Mann

SCALLOPS PROVENÇALE WITH PASTA AND AVOCADO

3 tablespoons light olive oil

3 tablespoons unsalted butter

1 pound trimmed and quartered sea scallops

8 minced shallots

8 minced green onions

2 minced large garlic cloves

2 teaspoons dried basil or 2 tablespoons minced fresh basil

1 teaspoon dried tarragon or 2 tablespoons fresh tarragon

¼ teaspoon dried thyme or ¾ teaspoon minced fresh thyme

½ cup dry white wine

4 cups well-drained, crushed canned tomatoes or 10 large fresh tomatoes, peeled, seeded and chopped

½ cup whipping cream

2 teaspoons sugar or to taste
Salt and freshly ground pepper

1 pound freshly cooked linguine

1 peeled, seeded, and chopped large avocado

Heat oil and butter in large non-aluminum skillet over medium heat. Add scallops and sauté until barely firm, about 2 minutes. Using slotted spoon, transfer to mixing bowl. Increase heat to medium-high. Add shallots and onion and sauté until soft. Stir in garlic and herbs; cook 1 minute. Add wine and cook 2 minutes more. Stir in tomatoes. Increase heat to high and boil briefly until sauce is thick. Stir in cream and sugar and cook another 20 seconds. Season with salt and pepper. Add to scallops, mixing gently. Toss with hot pasta and divide evenly among serving plates. Top with avocado.

4 servings

Judy Kennedy

BARBECUE SHRIMP #1

5 pounds raw shrimp in shells
4 thinly sliced lemons
2 tablespoons Worcestershire sauce
2 sticks butter, cut into pats
¼-½ bottle cracked black pepper
2 pods garlic
Salt to taste
¼ cup Italian dressing
3 green onions

Wash shrimp and place in Pyrex dish or roaster. Cover with pats of butter and lemon. Mix other ingredients and pour on top. Place under broiler until shrimp begin to turn pink. Turn oven to 350 degrees and cook until done, about 20 minutes. Serve with plenty of French bread for dipping.

Jennifer B. Briggs

BARBECUE SHRIMP #2

5 pounds large headless shrimp, in hull (15-20 count per pound)
1 pound melted butter
4 pods crushed garlic
3 bay leaves
1 tablespoon oregano
1 teaspoon rosemary
1 teaspoon barbecue spice
Salt, black pepper to taste
½ cup Chardonnay wine

Place shrimp in melted butter. Add all other ingredients. Place cover on pot and cook for 15 minutes. Remove cover and cook 15 minutes. Let it sit for 10 minutes before serving. Serve with hot New Orleans French bread to dip in sauce.

Kathleen V. Rudick

GARLIC SHRIMP WITH PESTO SAUCE

For Shrimp:

1 pound medium shrimp, deveined
¾ stick of butter
½ bunch green onions
4 chopped cloves garlic
Vermicelli noodles

In a large skillet melt butter, add garlic and green onion. Sauté until tender. Add shrimp and cook until bright pink. Spoon shrimp mixture over cooked Vermicelli and top with Pesto sauce and fresh Parmesan.

Pesto Sauce:

½ cup minced parsley
1 teaspoon dried or fresh basil
1 cup ricotta cheese
½ cup grated Parmesan cheese
½ cup pine nuts
2 chopped cloves garlic
¼ teaspoon salt
3 tablespoons olive oil

Blend above ingredients in blender. Add 3 tablespoons of olive oil and blend until smooth.

Serves 4

Ann Dickens

MICROWAVE BARBECUED SHRIMP

3 sticks melted margarine
2 tablespoons Worcestershire sauce
1 tablespoon hot sauce
½ cup freshly squeezed lemon juice
1½ tablespoons paprika
½ tablespoon garlic salt
1½ tablespoons barbecue powder
1 teaspoon salt
2½ pounds jumbo shrimp

Using a wire whisk, combine the melted margarine, Worcestershire, hot sauce, lemon juice, paprika, garlic salt, barbecue powder, and salt. Arrange shrimp in a shallow microwave safe glass dish. Pour sauce over the shrimp and cover with plastic wrap. Microwave on high for a total of 8 minutes, stopping to stir at 2 minute intervals. Serve with a green salad and lots of French bread to sop up the sauce!

Margaret Trahan

SHRIMP ANGEL HAIR PASTA

½ pound peeled, deveined
  and butterflied large
  shrimp
2 tablespoons olive oil
2 teaspoons minced garlic
1 teaspoon dried basil
½ teaspoon salt

¼ teaspoon pepper
½ cup seafood stock (made
  by boiling shrimp shells,
  strained) or chicken broth
½ cup white wine
1 chopped medium tomato

Place olive oil in large saucepan. Add garlic and shrimp and sauté about 2 minutes on medium heat or until shrimp are pink. Add tomato, basil, salt and pepper. Cook 1 minute. Add wine and stock. Heat thoroughly. Serve on top of angel hair pasta. Garnish with chopped fresh parsley.

2 servings

Lois J. Roy

SHRIMP AND ASPARAGUS IN CREAM SAUCE

¾-1 pound fresh asparagus
1 pound peeled, deveined
  shrimp
4 tablespoons unsalted
  butter
2 tablespoons flour

2 cups heavy whipping
  cream, heated
Salt
White pepper
Nutmeg
Noodles, lightly buttered

Rinse asparagus thoroughly. Break off tough bottoms. If thick peel stems. Blanch in boiling salted water until tender-crisp. Cut into 2-inch pieces. Melt 2 tablespoons butter in skillet. Sauté lightly salted shrimp until cooked but still crisp. Drain and save the juice. Melt 2 tablespoons butter in skillet. Add flour and whisk 3 minutes over heat until pale yellow. Add 2 cups heated cream. Bring sauce to a boil, whisking constantly. Season with pinch of nutmeg. Add asparagus and shrimp to sauce and heat, stirring constantly. Add salt and pepper, to taste. If sauce becomes too thick, add enough shrimp liquid to reach desired consistency. Serve over lightly buttered noodles.

Serves 4

Beth Landry

SHRIMP BAR-B-Q (MICROWAVE)

½ cup margarine
½ cup olive oil
1 tablespoon soy sauce
1 juice of lemon
2 bay leaves
1 tablespoon black pepper
¾ teaspoon cayenne pepper
½ teaspoon paprika
⅛ teaspoon rosemary
⅛ teaspoon thyme
⅛ teaspoon oregano
2 pounds unpeeled large shrimp
1 ½ teaspoons salt

Combine all ingredients except shrimp and salt in an 11 x 7 inch baking dish. Microwave (high—100%) for 2 to 3 minutes or until butter is melted. Add shrimp; mix lightly to coat with butter. Microwave (high—100%) for 8 to 9 minutes or until shrimp are tender; stirring once or twice. Stir in salt. Serve with French bread.

Serves 5

Jeannie Simon

SHRIMP AND EGGPLANT

3 eggplants, peeled and cubed
1 finely chopped large onion
2 minced large cloves garlic
¼ cup finely chopped red bell pepper
2 finely chopped ribs celery
2 tablespoons butter
2 tablespoons olive oil
3 cups shelled raw shrimp
2-3 tablespoons green onion tops
2-3 tablespoons parsley
Salt, pepper, red pepper or Creole seasoning to taste
½-¾ can condensed shrimp soup
¾ cup Italian bread crumbs

Peel eggplant and cut into cubes. Sprinkle salt on eggplant and soak 30 minutes. Drain. Steam eggplant until tender. Mash slightly. Sauté vegetables in butter and olive oil until soft. Add eggplant, shrimp, seasonings and cook stirring often, about 10 minutes. Add shrimp soup, onion tops, parsley and bread crumbs. Pour into an oblong Pyrex dish. Bake at 350 degrees until hot.

Marianne Schneider

SHRIMP LINGUINI

¼ pound butter or margarine
1 large onion
2 stalks celery
2 cloves garlic
½ cup green onions
½ cup bell pepper
1-2 pounds peeled raw shrimp
4 tablespoons flour

2 cups chicken broth
2 chicken bouillon cubes
Salt, pepper and Tabasco to taste
Parsley (optional)
½-1 pack linguini noodles, cooked

Chop vegetables fine and sauté in butter 15-30 minutes. Add shrimp and sauté until pink. Stir in flour and continue stirring for 3 minutes. Add chicken broth and bouillon cubes. Simmer 10-15 minutes. Add salt, pepper and Tabasco to taste. Add parsley. Serve over cooked linguini noodles.

4-6 servings

DeeAnne Jewell

SHRIMP RÉMOULADE

1 pound package (or 2 cans) deveined shrimp
1 finely chopped clove garlic
⅓ cup Kraft horseradish mustard
2 tablespoons paprika
2 tablespoons ketchup

½ teaspoon red pepper
1 teaspoon salt
⅓ cup tarragon vinegar
½ cup olive or salad oil
¼-½ cup finely chopped green onions and tops
¼-½ cup finely chopped celery

Mix ingredients and chill overnight. Serve over lettuce or can use as a dip with good crackers.

Dot Searcy

SHRIMP AND PASTA

3 (9 ounce) packages of soft linguini or a combination of linguine and angel hair (found in refrigerator section of market)

3 cans of chicken broth or 8-9 cups of homemade chicken broth

5 cups water

½ cup butter

1 small chopped green pepper or two green peppers if the red and yellow peppers are not available

1 small chopped red pepper

1 small chopped yellow pepper

1 small diced banana pepper

1 clove diced garlic

6 chopped green onions

3 stalks chopped celery

½ cup sliced fresh mushrooms (optional)

1 teaspoon salt

1 teaspoon seasoned pepper

½ teaspoon white pepper

1 teaspoon Creole seasoning

¼ teaspoon Tabasco sauce

2 teaspoons white wine Worcestershire sauce

1 teaspoon Worcestershire sauce

Juice of 1 large lemon

3 pounds of peeled shrimp

1 package of pasta prima Alfredo sauce blend

¾ cup milk

½ cup sour cream (optional)

2 tablespoons chopped parsley

1-2 (2.75 ounce) packages of grated three cheese (mozzarella, provolone and Romano)

Bring the chicken broth and water to a rapid boil in a large saucepan. Add the linguine and cook until tender, be careful not to over cook. Turn off heat and let the pasta absorb the rest of the broth. Melt the butter also in a large saucepan. Add the chopped peppers, green onion, celery, and garlic. Sauté until soft, add the fresh mushrooms if desired. Add salt, seasoned pepper, white pepper, Creole seasoning, Tabasco sauce, Worcestershire sauce. Add the shrimp and sauté until pink and tender (5-10 minutes). Add lemon juice and the package of Alfredo sauce, mix well add the milk and if desired the sour cream. Toss the linguine into the shrimp mixture. Add the grated three cheese package and the parsley. Toss well. Pour mixture into a 3 quart oblong Pyrex dish. If desired sprinkle another grated three cheese package on top. When ready to serve, heat at 350 degrees until hot and cheese has melted.

Marianne Schneider

SHRIMP AND SPINACH CASSEROLE

Mix together:

1 tablespoon olive oil	½ cup milk
1 stick butter	1 can cream of shrimp soup
1 (8 ounce) package soft cream cheese	

Mix separately:

3 (10 ounce) packages frozen chopped spinach, drain and squeeze out excess water	2 slices American cheese
	2 cups bread crumbs
	1½-2 pounds raw peeled small or medium shrimp
1 large can chopped artichoke hearts (drain and chop into bite size pieces)	Garlic powder to taste
	Salt and other seasonings to taste

Combine first 2 mixtures. Using two 8½-inch square aluminum cake pans, divide mixture evenly between the two pans. Break up cheese into small pieces and place on top of mixture and punch down into mixture with the handle of a wooden spoon.

Topping:

1 stick butter	Bacon bits
1 cup bread crumbs	

Topping: Melt one stick of butter and add 1 cup of bread crumbs. Divide this mixture between the pans and spread on top. Sprinkle bacon bits on top. Cover with foil and bake for 30 minutes at 350 degrees.

Could substitute a vegetable for shrimp.

Each pan serves 6 to 8 people

Lise Anne Dumond Slatten

SHRIMP SALAD JOAQUIN

1 pound cooked and cleaned shrimp	3 teaspoons chicken bouillon
1 cup chopped green onions	1 teaspoon red pepper
2 tablespoons olive oil	1 cup rice
3 minced garlic cloves	2 chopped tomatoes
2 cups water	1 chopped bell pepper
½ teaspoon Tabasco	

In large bowl, combine shrimp, onions, garlic and oil. Cover and refrigerate overnight. Cook rice in water with bouillon, hot sauce, and red pepper for 20 minutes. Let cool. Add tomatoes and bell peppers. Add rice mixture to shrimp mixture. Refrigerate until chilled.

6 servings

Kari Jordan

QUICK AND EASY TUNA CASSEROLE

2 cups finely broken tortilla chips (Doritos, Tostitos)	2 chopped jalapeño peppers (optional)
1 small can tuna in spring water, drained	1 can cream of mushroom soup
1 small chopped onion	Grated cheddar cheese

In a 2 quart casserole dish, sprayed with Pam, break into fine pieces Tostito chips. Spread drained tuna over the chips. In a small skillet, sauté onions and jalapeños until wilted and clear. Season vegetables generously with salt, red and black pepper and garlic powder. Spread onion mixture over tuna. Spread entire can of mushroom soup over onions to edges of dish. Cover with grated cheese. Bake at 350 degrees until sides are bubbly and cheese is melted. (15-20 minutes). Remove from oven and stir until everything is mixed well. Add more cheese to cover again. Place back in oven until cheese is melted. Ready to serve with additional chips.

Annette Bradley

© FLOYD SONNIER '85

CAJUN PRALINES

On a cold, rainy Sunday afternoon, my Mom would heat up her old black cast-iron skillet and roast peanuts to make her delicious cane-syrup and peanut pralines. We grew our own peanuts and made our own syrup from sugar cane we grew. We always had plenty of both on hand.

Mom would cook the syrup until it would become "candied". She would then add the roasted peanuts and mix well. On brown bagging paper, she would spoon the warm mixture into small pieces and let cool. I can still taste those wonderful sweet morsels of pralines.

Mom would also make popcorn pralines and pecan pralines.

Floyd Sonnier

PRALINES

When I was six or seven years old, my father ran for public office, so my grandmother would baby-sit while my parents were out campaigning. The hour of 9 p.m. was past my bed time, by parental decree. But my grandmother chose to disregard that decree, because that was when she felt it was time to make pralines. I felt my presence in the kitchen was necessary, even though I should have been in bed, because I had a very important task to perform. It was my job to tear off the wax paper and spread it on the counter, so Grandmother could drop the pralines on it.

What a wonderful memory, and what a wonderful knack my grandmother had for making a little girl feel like she was needed for the task of preparing a wonderful taste treat and was included in a conspiracy-of-sorts against my parents' curfew.

DESSERTS

CAKES

COOKIES

CANDY

PIES

GENERAL DESSERTS

AUNT DOODIE'S CHOCOLATE CAKE

1 box yellow pudding cake
mix
1 small box chocolate fudge
instant pudding
1 cup sour cream

1 cup oil
3 eggs
1 (6 ounce) package
chocolate chips

Mix all ingredients except chips. Grease a bundt cake pan and put 6 heaping tablespoons of batter on bottom. Sprinkle ½ of the chocolate chips on top of this. Add rest of batter and then other ½ of chips. Bake at 350 degrees for 50 minutes. May look wet when it comes out of oven.

After a beautiful day boating on False River, our friend made this delicious cake. My kids now ask me to fix it quite often.

Cheryl Ottinger

CHEESECAKE JULIET

Crust:

1 cup crumbled vanilla
wafers
½ cup chopped pecans

½ stick butter, melted
½ cup sugar

Mix all of the above and spread on bottom of buttered 10 inch springform pan.

Filling:

3 (8-ounce) packages cream
cheese
1 cup sugar

4 eggs
2 teaspoons vanilla

Break up cream cheese (softened) into chunks and mix with beaters on low speed, slowly adding sugar a little at a time. Add one egg at a time and beat well on medium speed. Add vanilla and beat at high speed for 1 minute. Pour over crust and bake at 350 degrees for 40 minutes. Remove cake from oven and turn up oven to 475 degrees.

Topping:

1 (8-ounce) carton sour
cream

3 tablespoons sugar
1 teaspoon vanilla

Mix well and pour over cake after it has cooled 5 minutes. Put cake back into oven and bake 5 more minutes. After cake has cooked 45 minutes, top with a fruit filling, if desired.

Juliet T. McKay

CAJUN CAKE

Cake:

1 (15½ ounce) can crushed pineapple
½ cup softened butter or margarine
1½ cups sugar

2 eggs
2 cups all-purpose flour
2 teaspoons baking powder
½ teaspoon baking soda
¼ teaspoon salt

Drain pineapple, reserving ½ cup juice. Set aside. Cream ½ cup softened butter; gradually add 1½ cups sugar, beating well at medium speed of an electric mixer. Add eggs, one at a time, beating well after each addition. Combine flour, baking powder, soda and salt; add to creamed mixture alternately with reserved juice, beginning and ending with flour mixture. Mix just until blended after each addition. Stir in crushed pineapple. Pour batter into a greased and floured 10 inch bundt pan. Bake at 350 degrees for 50 minutes or until wooden pick inserted in center comes out clean. Cool in pan 10 minutes; remove from pan and place on serving plate.

Topping:

¼ cup butter or margarine
½ cup sugar
⅓ cup evaporated milk
½ cup flaked coconut (toasted if desired)
½ cup chopped pecans
½ teaspoon vanilla extract

Toasted flaked coconut (optional garnish)
Pineapple slices (optional garnish)
Fresh pineapple leaves (optional garnish)

Combine ¼ cup butter and next four ingredients in small saucepan. Bring to a boil; reduce heat, simmer for 3 minutes. Stir in vanilla. Spoon on top of warm cake. Cool. Sprinkle with toasted coconut and garnish with pineapple slices and fresh leaves.

1 10 inch cake

Bettye Walker

CHOCOLATE ICE BOX CAKE

3 (4-ounce) German sweet
   chocolate bars
3 tablespoons water
3 tablespoons confectioner's
   sugar

6 separated eggs
2 dozen lady fingers
¾ cup chopped pecans
1 teaspoon vanilla extract
1 cup marshmallow tidbits

Melt chocolate with sugar and water in double boiler. Beat egg yolks lightly; fold in chocolate mixture and cool. Egg yolks should be room temperature so they won't "cook" when the hot chocolate mixture is added. Beat egg whites stiff, not dry, and fold into first mixture. Add vanilla, chopped nuts and marshmallows. Line sides and bottom of 8 inch spring form pan with split lady fingers. Alternate layers of chocolate mixture with remaining split lady fingers. Decorate with whipped cream or frozen whipped topping after removing cake from the spring form, or garnish with chopped pecans. This cake may also be prepared in square or oblong Pyrex dish and cut in squares to be iced with whipped cream.

12 servings

Elizabeth Bourque Preis

FRANGELICO CAKE

1 package butter recipe
   golden cake mix
1 regular size instant vanilla
   pudding mix
1 stick butter
4 eggs

¾ cup milk
⅓-½ cup hazelnut (Frangelico)
   liqueur
½ cup chopped pecans-cut
   fine and put at the bottom
   of the bundt pan

Have butter at room temperature. Mix cake mix and pudding mix. Add other ingredients and beat four minutes until smooth. Bake in greased bundt pan at 350 degrees for 1 hour or until done. When cake is cool, sprinkle with confectioner's sugar.

You can also sprinkle hazelnuts on bottom of pan.

Mary Blanchet Prejean

FRESH APPLE CAKE

3 cups flour
½ teaspoon salt
1 teaspoon baking soda
½ teaspoon cinnamon

½ teaspoon allspice
½ teaspoon nutmeg
½ teaspoon cloves

Sift together dry ingredients.

Egg mixture:

2 eggs
2 cups sugar

2 tablespoons vanilla
1 ½ cups vegetable oil

Mix egg mixture well. Add dry ingredients to mixture; mix well. Mix in apple mixture, stirring with large spoon.

Apple mixture:

3 cups finely chopped
   peeled apples

1 cup pecans

Bake in greased and floured bundt tube pan at 325 degrees for 1 hour and 20 minutes. Let cool in pan.

Leisa H. Comeaux

HEALTHFUL APPLE CAKE

⅔ cup sugar
½ cup packed brown sugar
¼ cup oil
3 egg whites
⅔ cup all-purpose flour
⅔ cup whole wheat flour

½ cup oat bran
1 ½ teaspoons baking soda
1 teaspoon cinnamon
¼ teaspoon allspice
3 cups unpeeled shredded
   apples

Spray 13 x 9 x 2 inch pan with nonstick spray. In large bowl combine sugars, oil and egg whites. Beat with wooden spoon until well blended. Add flours, oat bran, soda and spices; stir just until moistened. Stir in shredded apples. Spread into prepared pan. Bake at 350 degrees for 25 or 30 minutes. Cool in pan. Serve warm or cool.

Tina Roy

HISTORY OF THE KING CAKE

In European countries, the coming of the wise men bearing gifts to the Christ Child is celebrated twelve days after Christmas. The celebration, called Epiphany, Little Christmas or the Twelfth Night, is a time of exchanging gifts and feasting.

All over the world people gather for festive twelfth night celebrations. One of the most popular customs is still the baking of a special cake in honor of the three kings..."A King's Cake".

The Europeans

Continued on next page

KING'S CAKE

Brioche Dough:

½ cup lukewarm water (110 degrees to 115 degrees)
2 packages dry yeast
4½-5½ cups sifted flour
½ cup sugar
½ teaspoon freshly grated nutmeg
2 teaspoons salt
1 teaspoon grated lemon rind
½ cup lukewarm milk
3 eggs
4 egg yolks
½ cup + 2 tablespoons butter, softened
1 egg lightly beaten with 1 tablespoon milk
1 dime or uncooked dried bean or miniature doll

Soften yeast in water. Combine flour, sugar, nutmeg and salt in mixing bowl. Stir in lemon peel. Make a well in center and pour into it the yeast mixture and milk. Add eggs and egg yolks, and with a large wooden spoon gradually incorporate dry ingredients into liquid ones. Beat in butter and continue beating until dough forms ball. (Mixing of the dough can be done in food processor.) Place ball on floured board and incorporate more flour if necessary, by sprinkling it over ball by the tablespoon. Knead until smooth and elastic. Brush inside of large bowl with 1 tablespoon softened butter. Set dough in bowl and turn it so as to butter entire surface. (At this point you can refrigerate dough overnight.) Cover bowl and set aside for 1½ hours or until doubled in bulk. Brush a large baking sheet with remaining butter. Punch dough down on lightly floured surface. Knead, then pat and shape dough into a cylinder about 14 inches long. Place on baking sheet and form into a ring. Press bean or

hide a bean inside their cake and the person receiving the bean must portray one of the kings. Latin-American people put a small figure inside the cake representing the Christ Child. It is said that a year of good fortune awaits the lucky person who gets the figure.

King's Cake (continued)

dime or doll into dough so that it is hidden. Set aside again to rise. When ready to bake brush the top and sides of the ring with the egg-milk mixture. Bake King's Cake in middle of oven at 375 degrees for 25 to 30 minutes, or until golden brown. Slide cake onto wire rack to cool.

Sugars:

> Green, purple and yellow food coloring pastes
> 12 tablespoons granulated sugar

Prepare the colored sugars by squeezing a dab of paste into the palm of one hand. Sprinkle 2 tablespoons of sugar over the paste and rub your hands together to color the sugars evenly. Set aside and repeat process with green, then twice with purple and yellow. (Do not mix sugars.)

Icing:

> 3 cups confectioner's sugar
> ¼ cup strained fresh lemon juice
> 3-6 tablespoons water
> 2 candied cherries, halved lengthwise

When the cake has cooled, prepare the icing. Combine the confectioner's sugar, lemon juice and 3 tablespoons of water in a deep bowl and stir until the icing mixture is smooth. If too stiff to spread, beat in 1 teaspoonful water at a time, until desired consistency is reached. With a small metal spatula, spread the icing over the top of the cake, allowing it to run down the sides. Sprinkle the colored sugars over the icing immediately, forming a row of purple, yellow and green strips, each about 2 inches wide, on both sides of the ring. Arrange two cherry halves at each end of the cake, pressing them gently into the icing.

Do not use liquid food coloring as it will make the sugar dissolve.

Louisianians like the idea of perpetuating the celebration by having the person who received the baby continue the festivities with another party and another cake. Starting the twelfth day after Christmas, King Cake Parties continue until the first day of Lent, ending on Fat Tuesday, Mardi Gras! King Cakes were originally a simple ring of dough with little decoration. The South

Continued on next page

Louisiana style King Cake is brightly decorated with colored sugars in Mardi Gras colors of purple, green and gold.

Thousands of King Cakes are consumed at parties every year making the King Cake another "Fine Louisiana Tradition".

In my family, there is a tradition of naming babies after their relatives. Our family includes Leopold, Jr., Leopold III, Leopold IV, Big Fay, Little Fay, Big Jeanne and Li'l Jeanne.

Another tradition is making special occasions REALLY special. We go all out to celebrate everything— particularly birthdays. At each birthday celebration, the honoree is allowed to choose the dinner menu. Li'l Jeanne's choice always included fried chicken, pea salad, Macque Choux, croissants and a deadly chocolate cake.

I enjoy sharing the memories of so many special occasions, and sharing the recipe for Li'l Jeanne's Birthday Cake.

LI'L JEANNE'S BIRTHDAY CAKE

Step I:
    2 cups sugar
    2 cups flour

Combine in a large mixing bowl.

Step II:
    ½ cup cooking oil
    1 stick margarine
    1 cup water
    3 tablespoons unsweetened cocoa

Combine with dry mixture in mixing bowl. Beat at low speed for 1 minute.

Step III:
    2 eggs
    ½ cup buttermilk
    1 tablespoon vanilla
    1 teaspoon baking soda

Take 2 eggs and beat well. Mix into bowl ½ cup buttermilk and 1 tablespoon vanilla extract. Add to other ingredients. Sprinkle 1 teaspoon of baking soda over mixture. Mix one minute. Pour into 11 x 8 x 2 inch pan and bake at 400 degrees for about 20 minutes. Ice while hot.

Icing:
    1 stick margarine
    6 tablespoons Pet milk
    3 tablespoons unsweetened cocoa
    1 box confectioner's sugar
    1 tablespoon vanilla extract

Bring first 3 ingredients to a boil in a saucepan. Pour into mixing bowl and add confectioner's sugar and extract. Beat until smooth and creamy. Pour over hot cake and let cool.

Fay Bowen

PINEAPPLE DELIGHT

1 (15-ounce) can crushed
pineapple
1 large Sara Lee pound
cake

1 small container frozen
whipped topping
1 (3-4 ounce) box vanilla
Jello instant pudding mix
1 teaspoon almond extract

Drain juice off of pineapple. Mix box of pudding with pineapple and almond extract. Fold in cool whip. Cut pound cake into 3 levels lengthwise. Layer pineapple mixture over each level of cake and smooth around top and sides. Chill for 1 hour.

This recipe is so delicious and so easy to make. It is great for a last minute dessert when company is coming over.

Cheryl Ottinger

PRALINE CHEESECAKE

1¼ cups crushed graham
crackers
¼ cup granulated sugar
¼ cup toasted chopped
pecans
¼ cup melted butter
3 (8-ounce) packages
softened cream cheese
1 cup packed brown sugar
1 (5⅓ ounce) can (⅔ cup)
evaporated milk

2 tablespoons all-purpose
flour
1½ teaspoons vanilla
3 eggs
1 cup toasted pecan halves
1 cup dark corn syrup
¼ cup cornstarch
2 tablespoons brown sugar
1 teaspoon vanilla

In small mixing bowl, combine cracker crumbs, granulated sugar and chopped pecans. Stir in the melted butter. Press crumb mixture over the bottom and 1½ inches up the sides of a 9 inch springform pan. Bake in 350 degree oven for 10 minutes. Meanwhile beat together cream cheese, brown sugar, evaporated milk, flour and vanilla. Add eggs, beat until just blended. Pour into baked crust. Bake in 350 degree oven for 50 to 55 minutes or until set. Cool in pan 30 minutes, loosen sides and remove rim from pan. Cool completely. Arrange nut halves atop cheesecake. Before serving, combine corn syrup, cornstarch and the remaining brown sugar in a small saucepan. Cook and stir until thickened and bubbly. Remove from heat, stir in the vanilla. Cool slightly. To serve, spoon some of the warm sauce over the nuts on the cheesecake. Pass remaining sauce.

12 to 16 servings

Allison Bean

All five children in my family loved my mother's Scotch Cake. She was never surprised, when one of us had a birthday, that we requested it as the birthday cake. My younger brother, Pat, did surprise her on one of his birthdays, however. We had planned no party, because relatives were visiting from out of town, and we decided on a quiet family celebration of his birthday. But Pat made a different decision. Without mentioning it to the family, he invited his entire second grade class to our house after school to help him celebrate eight years on this earth.

It was April Fool's Day, so when my mother learned of it, there was some hope that it was a joke. It wasn't. As Pat's classmates began arriving, she dashed off to the bakery. It is the only birthday I can recall that we did not celebrate with my mother's wonderful Scotch Cake.

SCOTCH CAKE

Sift the following ingredients:
 2 cups flour
 2 cups sugar
 4 tablespoons cocoa
Mix:
 1 cup water
 1 stick margarine
 1 stick butter

Heat until the butter melts and add to dry mixture.
Add:
 2 eggs lightly beaten
 ½ cup buttermilk
 1 teaspoon baking soda
 1 teaspoon vanilla extract

Mix together. Spray bundt pan with Pam and bake at 400 degrees for twenty minutes. Cool on a wire rack.
Icing:
 1 stick margarine, melted
 1 box powdered sugar
 4 tablespoons cocoa
 6 tablespoons milk
 1 tablespoon vanilla
 1 cup chopped pecans

Mix together and pour icing over hot cake. Don't wait for a birthday, this is good for any occasion. Just make sure you have the necessary ingredients and at least 45 minutes to prepare this cake!

Miriam Bourgeois

There is a cake that has special memories attached and has achieved a measure of fame in my neighborhood. It calls up memories of special weekends for the children, car-pooling for baseball games and new neighbors. Sour Cream Coffee Cake was always a part of such events. It was a gift to the families who invited the children to spend a weekend, a way of saying thanks for the shared transportation to the games and a welcoming gift to new people in the neighborhood. And—when it was time for the children to return to college after a weekend at home—it was always there for the trip.

SOUR CREAM COFFEE CAKE

Cake:
- 1 box butter recipe cake mix
- ½ cup sugar
- ½ cup cooking oil
- 1 (8-ounce) carton sour cream
- 5 eggs
- 3 tablespoons light brown sugar
- 2 teaspoons cinnamon
- 1 tablespoon sugar
  Butter flavored vegetable oil or shortening

Blend cake mix, sugar, oil and sour cream. Add eggs one at a time, beating well after each, on medium speed. Place half of the cake batter into greased and sugar sprinkled bundt pan. Sprinkle the mix of brown sugar and cinnamon on top of the batter, trying to keep it almost in the middle of the batter, not touching the sides of the pan. Cover with the remainder of the batter. Bake 350 degrees for 50 minutes. Test with a cake tester to make sure the center of the cake is done. Let cake sit in pan for 10 minutes before inverting on the cake plate.

Glaze:
- 1 cup powdered sugar
- 1 tablespoon melted butter
- 1 tablespoon milk
- 1 teaspoon vanilla

When the cake is still warm, pour the glaze all over. A little more milk may be needed to make glaze drizzle easier. Rum may be substituted for vanilla.

Serves 12

Carol Ann Roberts Dumond

TURTLE CHIP CAKE

Cake:

1 box German chocolate or
Swiss chocolate cake mix
½ cup margarine
1 cup water
1 cup vegetable oil
3 eggs

1 can condensed milk,
divided into 2 equal parts
1 package caramel candy
(14 ounce)
1 cup chopped pecans

Cream margarine into cake mix. Add water, oil, eggs and ½ can condensed milk. Pour half of batter into greased and floured 9 x 13 inch pan. Bake at 350 degrees for 30 minutes. While cake bakes, melt caramels and remaining ½ can condensed milk. Stir in pecans and spread over hot cake. Add remaining cake batter and bake another 30 minutes.

Icing:

½ cup margarine
6 tablespoons milk
1 package small chocolate
chips

3 tablespoons cocoa
1 box confectioner's sugar
½ cup chopped pecans

Melt margarine with cocoa, milk and sugar. Beat well. Pour icing over hot cake. Sprinkle with pecans and chocolate chips.

Teri Broussard - Iris Wiederhold

CHOCOLATE GRAHAM CRACKER BARS

12 double graham crackers
1 cup butter
1 cup light brown sugar

1 (11-ounce) package milk
chocolate chips
1 cup chopped pecans

Line a jelly roll or metal pan with foil. Place graham crackers on foil. Melt butter and light brown sugar. Boil 3 minutes - be sure to boil - not cook - 3 minutes, stirring constantly. Should be thick. Pour over graham crackers and spread evenly. Bake at 400 degrees for 5 minutes. Watch closely so it does not burn. Sprinkle milk chocolate chips (must be milk chocolate) over sugar-butter mixture and spread until even. Sprinkle pecans over melted chocolate. Cut into squares.

Jean Frazell

Most people have poignant memories of Easter time and the fun of dyeing the eggs. In my family, there was a similar experience at Christmas Time. Preparations for the Season were not complete until the Christmas cookies were baked and iced. The children in the family were part of this Yuletide family tradition. We helped by rolling and cutting the dough, but the real joy came in icing the cookies in a myriad of colors and painting them. It was very special, not only to us children, but also to my Dad. I know that the Christmas tradition brought back rich memories of his childhood. Today, it is a food memory that calls up wonderful memories of my own.

CHRISTMAS COOKIES

Cookies:
- 3 eggs
- 2 sticks butter
- 2 cups sugar
- ½ cup evaporated milk
- 1 teaspoon soda
- 1 tablespoon almond extract or 2 teaspoons nutmeg and 1 ½ tablespoons vanilla extract
- 2 teaspoons baking powder
- 7½ cups flour

Beat eggs. Add butter, sugar, milk and mix. Mix soda in a little water (enough to stir) and add to mixture. Sift flour and baking powder together and blend gradually into cookie mixture. Grease and flour cookie sheets. Roll dough into ¼ inch thickness and cut with Christmas cookie cutters and place on cookie sheet. Bake at 375 degrees for 10 to 12 minutes.

Icing:
- 2 cups powdered sugar
- 3 tablespoons evaporated milk
- 1 teaspoon vanilla extract
- 1-3 drops food coloring

Sift powdered sugar and stir in milk until mixture reaches icing consistency. Add vanilla extract for flavor and stir. Divide icing into containers and add food coloring to each container to obtain desired colors. Ice cookies after they have cooled. Allow icing to dry before moving cookies.

5 dozen cookies

Kay Z. Marix

CROWNIES

2 cups flour
2 cups sugar
½ pound butter
¼ cup cocoa
1 cup water

2 eggs
½ cup buttermilk or sour cream
1 teaspoon baking soda
1 teaspoon vanilla

Mix flour and sugar together. Mix all other ingredients together and bring to a boil in pan. Mix all together and beat well. Pour in jelly roll pan that has been greased and lightly floured. Bake at 400 degrees for 20 minutes.

Frosting:

¼ pound butter
1 teaspoon vanilla
¼ cup cocoa

6 tablespoons evaporated milk
½ cup nuts (optional)
1 pound powdered sugar

Mix butter, vanilla, cocoa, milk and nuts together. Bring to a boil and pour mix over powdered sugar. Mix well. Frost cake warm.

Sara Hamsa

MARIONETTES

12 honey graham crackers
1-1½ cups chopped pecans
1 stick (¼ pound) oleo margarine

1 stick (¼ pound) butter
½ cup granulated sugar

Use a cookie sheet with sides. Heat oven to 325 degrees. Break graham crackers in half and half again (where scored) and line ungreased pan with crackers side by side. Pan should be lined completely with crackers. Sprinkle chopped pecans over all crackers. Melt butter and oleo in small saucepan. Add sugar and bring to a boil. Boil for 2 minutes, then dribble over all the crackers and pecans. Try to cover all of the crackers. Bake at 325 degrees for 18 minutes. Carefully remove from pan with spatula one cookie at a time, and place on waxed paper to cool. They will harden as they cool.

48 cookies

Marion Berry

KIFLEE

Dough:

2 cups flour
2 sticks margarine

1 (8-ounce) package
Philadelphia cream cheese

Mix above ingredients together. Gently knead dough. Break dough into 4 balls. Refrigerate dough so it will be firm when ready to roll. (May refrigerate overnight).

Filling:

1 pound finely ground
  pecans
2 cups sugar
1 cup milk

2 teaspoons flavoring -
  walnut or maple
1 stick of margarine

Mix sugar and milk over heat until dissolved. Add rest of ingredients until thoroughly mixed. Set aside. Dust flour and sugar on a board to ease dough rolling. Roll dough about pie crust thickness. Place a thin line of filling at one end and roll over. Cut rolled portion from rest of dough. Dip pastry brush into milk and coat roll. Mix together 1 cup sugar and 1 cup ground pecans. Sprinkle on top of roll. Cut roll into 2 inch strips. Place on greased cookie sheet. May be placed close together. Bake at 350 degrees for approximately 25 minutes. Repeat process until all dough is used. This freezes well.

9 to 10 dozen

Pat Low

MACAROONS

1⅓ cups sugar
3-4 tablespoons cocoa

3 large egg whites
3½ cups ground pecans

Beat egg whites until stiff. Mix sugar and cocoa. Add egg whites and pecans. Make little balls - roll in sugar. Place on cookie sheet with wax paper. Bake at 350 degrees for 15 minutes.

Makes 65 to 75

Ruth Sandlin

FORGOTTEN COOKIES

⅔ cup sugar
2 egg whites

1 cup chocolate chips
1 cup finely chopped pecans

Preheat oven to 350 degrees. Beat egg whites stiff, adding sugar slowly until eggs are stiff. Add pecans and chips. Drop on ungreased cookie sheet by 1 teaspoon per cookie. Place in oven and turn off heat. Leave in oven overnight or at least 4 hours.

6 dozen

Lisa Breaux

✎ ULTIMATE SOUR LEMON BARS

Crust:

1½ cups all purpose flour
¼ cup powdered sugar
Pinch of salt

½ cup (1 stick) chilled unsalted butter, cut into pieces
½ teaspoon vanilla extract

Preheat oven to 350 degrees. Butter bottom and sides of a 9 inch square baking pan. Combine flour, powdered sugar and salt in processor. Add butter and cut using on/off turns until mixture appears sandy. Add vanilla and process until dough begins to come together. Press dough evenly into prepared baking pan. Bake crust until golden brown, about 30 minutes.

Filling:

5 large eggs, room temperature
2 cups sugar
1 cup strained lemon juice

3 tablespoons all-purpose flour
Powdered sugar

Whisk eggs and 2 cups sugar in medium bowl to blend. Whisk in lemon juice, then all purpose flour. Strain into another bowl. Reduce oven temperature to 325 degrees. Pour filling over hot crust. Bake until sides are set and filling no longer moves in center when pan is shaken, about 20 minutes. Cover and chill at least 4 hours. Sprinkle with powdered sugar over squares before serving.

Allison Bean

To be considered delicious, food must customarily please the eye as well as the palate. In our family recipe box, there is an exception. We call the result achieved from this recipe "Sad Sack Cookies." They do not stand up smartly, but they go down easily, and so very pleasantly. The origin of the name was lost somewhere in the past, but the assumption is that, because they sink in the middle in a way that leaves them less than attractive, they look "sad."

But there is ample compensation for their forlorn appearance.

Such a sad face.

Such a happy taste.

NAN'S SAD COOKIES

2 cups biscuit mix
1 pound box brown sugar
4 eggs
⅓ cup vegetable oil
1 cup chopped pecans
1 teaspoon vanilla
⅓ cup golden raisins
⅓ cup mixed fruit (optional)

Mix all ingredients together and pour into 10 x 13 inch greased pan. Bake at 375 degrees for 35 to 40 minutes. Cool and cut into squares.

Noelie Dronet

NUTTY CHEESE BARS

Base:

1 box butter recipe golden
   cake mix
¾ cup melted butter or
   margarine

1½ cups chopped pecans
   (divided ¾ cup, ¾ cup)

Preheat oven to 350 degrees. Grease and flour pan 9 x 13 inch regular baking pan. Stir together cake mix, ¾ cup melted butter, ¾ cup pecans. Press evenly into bottom of pan.

Topping:

1 cup brown sugar, packed

2 (8 ounce) packages
   softened cream cheese

Stir together brown sugar and cream cheese. Spread evenly over the base in pan. Sprinkle with ¾ cup chopped pecans. Bake 25 to 30 minutes until edges are brown and cheese topping is set. Cool completely before cutting. Store in refrigerator in an airtight container.

Ann Marie Hightower

PEANUT BUTTER BROWNIES

⅓ cup butter
½ cup crunchy peanut butter
¾ cup light brown sugar
¾ cup granulated sugar
2 eggs
2 teaspoons vanilla

1 cup non-sifted flour
1 teaspoon baking soda
1 teaspoon salt
2 (6-ounce) packages
   chocolate morsels

Preheat oven to 350 degrees. Cream butter, peanut butter and sugars. Add eggs one at a time. Add vanilla. Mix thoroughly. Blend in dry ingredients. Stir in one package of chocolate morsels. Spread batter in nongreased 13 x 9 x 2 inch pan. Sprinkle second package of morsels on top. Bake for 2 minutes. Remove from oven and spread chocolate morsels on top to make a marbled icing. Bake an additional 28 minutes. Cool and cut into bars or squares.

2 dozen

Monique Gideon

Peanut Butter Oatmeal Cookies

½ cup margarine
½ cup milk
2 cups sugar
4 tablespoons cocoa

½ cup peanut butter
1 teaspoon vanilla
3 cups one-minute oatmeal

Melt margarine in pot. Add milk, sugar and cocoa. Boil for 1 minute then remove from heat. Add peanut butter and vanilla. Stir in oatmeal. Drop from teaspoon onto waxed paper. Cookies will harden when they cool.

3 dozen

Lee Ann Broussard

Pumpkin Nut Cookies

½ cup butter
1 cup sugar
2 beaten eggs
1 cup canned pumpkin
1 teaspoon vanilla
2 cups sifted flour

4 tablespoons baking powder
2½ teaspoons cinnamon
½ teaspoon nutmeg
¼ teaspoon ginger
1 cup raisins (if desired)
1 cup chopped nuts

Cream butter, add sugar gradually. Cream until light and fluffy. Add egg, vanilla and pumpkin. Mix well. Sift flour, baking powder and spices together. Stir in dry ingredients. Mix until blended. Add raisins and nuts. Drop teaspoonfuls on greased cookie sheet. Bake at 350 degrees for 15 minutes.

3 dozen

Marianne Schneider

Microwave Peanut Butter Fudge

2 cups sugar
2 cups firmly packed light brown sugar
1 cup evaporated milk
½ cup butter or margarine

1 cup peanut butter
1 (7 ounce) jar marshmallow creme
2 teaspoons vanilla

Combine first four ingredients in 2½ quart casserole dish. Microwave on high 13 minutes. Stir well at 4 minute intervals. Add remaining ingredients and stir until melted. Pour in buttered 13 x 9 inch dish. Chill at least 2 hours. Cut into 1 inch squares.

9 dozen 1-inch squares

Gloria Billeaud

The early Forties were a time of world conflict, but also a time of simple, innocent pastimes that are so pleasant to remember. I recall vividly those Friday night fudge parties with my girl friends. Rationing was in effect then because of the war, so we were each allowed to contribute one cup of sugar toward this rare treat.

I don't know if many kids would consider a fudge party so delightful these days, but if they did, the ingredients would certainly be more plentiful than during World War II. And, how easy it is now to make Divinity using a candy thermometer. Among my favorite memories is relying on the old way—the "cracking of the syrup" in a cup of cold water. It is a memory of a special time in America.

DIVINITY

1 cup water
5 cups sugar
1 cup light corn syrup
½ teaspoon salt
4 egg whites at room temperature
2 teaspoons vanilla extract or (1 teaspoon vanilla & 1 teaspoon almond extract)
1½ cups chopped pecans
¼ teaspoon green food color

Grease well 13 x 9 inch baking pan and line with foil; set aside. In large saucepan over medium heat, heat 5 cups sugar, 1 cup corn syrup, ½ teaspoon salt and 1 cup water to boiling, stirring constantly. With pastry brush dipped in hot water and drained, brush sides of pan to wash down any sugar crystals which form. Insert candy thermometer; continue cooking until temperature reaches 248 degrees Fahrenheit.

Meanwhile, in large bowl with mixer at high speed, beat 4 egg whites until stiff peaks form. Beating at high speed, slowly pour half of syrup into whites. Continue beating while heating other half of syrup to 278 degrees. Continue beating; slowly pour hot remaining syrup into mixture; beat until mixed and very stiff. Add vanilla extract and food coloring. Beat until mixed. Add chopped pecans and beat until mixed. Pour into 3 quart buttered Pyrex dish immediately. Let cool and cut into squares.

4 dozen

Mary Blanchet Prejean

During a certain season of every year, South Louisiana faces the possibility of a hurricane's onslaught. Hurricane Hilda, which roared up from the Gulf of Mexico in 1964, left behind extensive damage and the usual memories of anxiety and fear. But it also left me with one of my most precious food memories.

I was 11 years old then, and we lived in the small town of Crowley, in a raised cottage-type house. Dad boarded up the house completely as Hilda approached, and when the storm hit, we found ourselves without electricity. It was a killer storm with howling winds and rattling windows. But somehow, as we gathered in the living room with candles and kerosene lamps and played card games, I thought more of how cozy it was than how dangerous.

Perhaps the most memorable part of the experience was not the storm's attack, but the sudden decision of my Dad to whip up something on the stove, which was fueled by gas and still operable. My ten-year-old brother and six-year-old sister were as amazed as I was, because we had never seen our Dad cook. And even more amazing was the fact that this man who never allowed us late night snacks, was going to make fudge. We couldn't believe that he even knew how.

HURRICANE FUDGE

3 cups sugar
⅔ cup cocoa
⅛ teaspoon salt
1 ½ cups milk
¼ cup butter or margarine
1 teaspoon vanilla
½ cup chopped pecans

Combine sugar, cocoa, salt and milk in a large pot. Bring to a boil, stirring constantly over medium heat until it reaches a soft ball stage. Remove from heat. Add butter or margarine and cool mixture to 110 degrees in a pan of water. Add vanilla and chopped pecans. Beat until mixture loses its gloss (about 2 minutes). Pour onto a buttered plate. Slice into squares when cool.

Margaret H. Trahan

We crowded around the stove in our tiny kitchen, and soon an absolutely heavenly smell filled our home. It was the thrill of our young lives to enjoy an unexpected and forbidden treat, while a hurricane raged around our house. To this day, when the hurricane warnings are sounding in the media, I think back with great fondness to that night when Hilda struck, and Dad surprised and delighted us all. It is a beautiful memory.

PEANUT BUTTER BALLS

3 sticks whipped butter
1 ½ boxes powdered sugar
2 cups peanut butter

18 ounces chocolate chips
½ bar paraffin

Using your hands, mix the butter, powdered sugar and peanut butter together and form into balls. Put in freezer for at least an hour. When the balls are hard, then melt the chocolate chips and paraffin in a small pot. Using a toothpick, dip the balls into the melted chocolate mixture. Cool the candy on wax paper.

Makes wonderful gifts at Christmas!

Adam and Robin Trahan

BROWNIE PIE

1 stick oleo or butter
1 square unsweetened
  chocolate
1 cup sugar
½ cup sifted flour

2 eggs
½ teaspoon vanilla
¾ cup coarsely chopped
  pecans

Melt oleo with chocolate. Remove from heat and stir in sugar. Stir in flour and eggs. Add vanilla and pecans. Pour into a 9 inch pie plate that has been sprayed with Pam. Bake at 325 degrees for 25 to 30 minutes. Top with vanilla ice cream or chocolate sauce.

Serves 6

Patsy Glover McCord

BLACK BOTTOM PIE

2½ cups finely crumbled
   graham crackers
1 stick melted butter
2 cups whole milk or half &
   half
½ cup sugar
1¼ tablespoons cornstarch
4 large egg yolks
1 tablespoon gelatin

1¼ squares unsweetened
   chocolate
1 teaspoon vanilla
4 stiffly beaten egg whites
½ cup sugar
¼ teaspoon cream of tartar
1 teaspoon vanilla
1 pint whipping cream
Grated chocolate

Melt butter, mix well with graham cracker crumbs, press firmly on bottom and sides of 7½ x 12 inch dish. Bake at 275 degrees for 1 hour or until very crisp. Cool thoroughly. Separate eggs, put whites in mixing bowl. Set aside. Add hot milk, stir until well mixed, return to pot and cook until wooden spoon is well coated. Stir in gelatin which was soaked in ⅓ cup water. Divide custard in half. In one half add melted chocolate and vanilla. Stir thoroughly. Pour on top of crust. Refrigerate until "set". In other half, fold in stiffly beaten egg whites to which cream of tartar, sugar and vanilla have been added. Pour on top of cooled chocolate custard. Refrigerate. Beat cream. Put on top of custard after it has been thoroughly cooled and is firm. Grate unsweetened chocolate sparingly on top.

Serves 9

The first time I read this recipe written by "Miss Ruby" from Lake Providence, Louisiana she suggested that the cook place the custard directly "under the unit" to cool. This was a time when refrigerator's cooling elements were inside and were the coldest part. She also said to use a 10 cent box of vanilla wafers for the crust!

Phallie Evans

TRIP TO GRANDMA'S

My fondest childhood memories are of visits to my grandmother's home in Whiteville, Louisiana. Somehow, the memories are tied up with the good smells of her country home—like freshly mopped floors and rain water collected in a big bin. But the most memorable aroma of all was from Mom Mom's Custard Pies. They were a tradition with Sunday meals, and were served at every family get-together. Still today, birthdays, christenings, reunions and other events that bring us all together follow that tradition. Now in its fourth generation, the tradition is very precious to our family.

BOOIE PIE À LA BIG MOM

Dough:

2 cups sugar	2 tablespoons milk
1 stick butter or ½ cup cooking oil	3 teaspoons baking powder
	1¼ teaspoons baking soda
3 eggs	2 tablespoons vanilla
4 cups flour	

Mix ingredients and put dough in refrigerator overnight. Dough will be somewhat sticky. Take dough out a little before ready to use. Knead dough in flour a few strokes then place in 3 8-inch pie plates. Keep some dough for the covering of the pies.

Pie Filling:

3½ cups sugar	3 teaspoons vanilla
1 egg yolk	1½ cups flour
1 can Carnation milk	½ teaspoon nutmeg
1 can water	½ cup butter
¾ pint whole milk	

Put flour in a bowl using some of the above water (lukewarm). Form a paste, add egg yolk and nutmeg. Put aside. Place sugar in a big pot and brown until darkens on low heat. When brown, remove from heat and add remainder of above water. Be careful, it will make steam when water is added. Resume stirring over heat. Stir in all of the milk, stirring until all sugar rock is melted using low heat. Finally add flour mixture from above. Stir until thickens then add ½ cup of butter. Add filling to pie shells, top with extra dough and bake at 325 degrees for 45 minutes or until golden brown.

Tip: When browning sugar, tan only ⅓ and add rest slowly.

Yields 3 8-inch pies

Carl Thibodeaux

BUTTERMILK PIE

1 ⅓ cups sugar
  3 tablespoons flour
  2 beaten eggs
  1 stick melted butter
  1 cup buttermilk

2 teaspoons vanilla
1 teaspoon lemon extract
1 9 or 10 inch unbaked
  pastry shell

Combine sugar and flour. Beat eggs thoroughly and add to sugar-flour mixture. Add melted oleo and buttermilk. Mix well. Add extracts. Pour into chilled deep dish 9 or 10 inch unbaked pastry shell. Bake at 350 degrees for 45 minutes without opening door.

Dot Searcy

CHOCOLATE CREAM CHEESE PIE

Crust:

½ cup chopped pecans
1 cup sifted flour

⅛ teaspoon salt
1 stick melted butter

Mix together and press into regular pie plate. Bake at 350 degrees for 15 minutes. Make crust and cool.

First Layer:

1 (8 ounce) package
  softened cream cheese
1 cup sifted powdered sugar

1 teaspoon vanilla
1 cup frozen whipped
  topping

Mix together first 3 ingredients then fold in whipped topping. Put into pie pan.

Second Layer:

1 (4 ounce) package instant
  chocolate pudding mix

1 ½ cups milk
1 teaspoon vanilla

Mix together all ingredients. Put on top of first layer. Top whole pie with more whipped topping.

Terri Foret

CONDENSED MILK PIE

Crust:

1 box of vanilla wafers, crushed

⅓ melted bar of real butter

Mix and press into 9 inch pie plate.

Filling:

1 can sweet condensed milk

2-3 egg yolks

1 teaspoon vanilla

1 cup pecans

Cook in double boiler until thick. Add 1 cup pecans. Pour mixture in vanilla wafer crust and refrigerate until cool. Top with whipped cream or light whipped topping.

8 servings

This recipe is a dessert from Arthur Randol's family reunion of 100 each July 4th weekend on the Guadalupe River in New Braunfels, Texas (30 miles out of San Antonio). The Mexican food served is always catered followed by this very rich dessert. For a large crowd, make several recipes in 9 x 12 inch Pyrex dish. Keep refrigerated until served.

Lucile Randol

CRANBERRY CREAM PIE

1 (16 ounce) can whole berry cranberry sauce

¼ cup sugar

1 envelope unflavored gelatin

2 tablespoons orange juice

½ teaspoon grated orange peel

1 cup whipping cream, whipped

1 9 inch graham cracker pie crust

Whipped cream, if desired

In medium saucepan, combine cranberry sauce and sugar; bring to boil. In a small dish, sprinkle gelatin over orange juice, stir and let stand for 1 minute so gelatin can soften. Remove cranberry mixture from heat; stir in gelatin and orange peel. Cool to room temperature. Fold whipped cream into cranberry mixture. Pour into pie crust. Chill until firm, about 2 hours. Serve with additional whipped cream, if desired.

Tina Roy

COUNTRY APPLE PIE

Crust:
   2 unbaked 9 inch pie crusts

Nut Filling:
   1 ½ cups chopped pecans
   2 tablespoons firmly packed
      brown sugar
   1 tablespoon milk
   2 tablespoons beaten egg
   ¼ teaspoon vanilla
   ¼ teaspoon fresh lemon juice
   1 tablespoon butter or
      margarine, softened

Preheat oven to 425 degrees. Combine nuts, brown sugar, milk, egg, vanilla, lemon juice and butter. Spread evenly over bottom of unbaked pie shell.

Apple Filling:
   2 (21 ounce) cans apple pie
      filling
   1 teaspoon fresh lemon juice
   ¾ cup granulated sugar
   2 tablespoons all-purpose
      flour
   1 teaspoon cinnamon
   2 tablespoons butter

Place apple filling in large bowl. Sprinkle with lemon juice. Combine granulated sugar, flour and cinnamon. Sprinkle over apple filling. Toss to coat. Spoon over nut filling. Dot with butter. Moisten pastry edge with water. Lift top crust onto filled pie. Fold top edge under bottom crust. Flute edges. Cut slits in top crust for escape of steam. Put pie on cookie sheet when baking — could be messy while baking. Bake for 50 minutes. Cover edge of pie with foil, removing foil after baking 30 minutes. Cool until barely warm or to room temperature before serving. Top with whipped cream or vanilla ice cream.

                                                 Lise Anne Dumond Slatten

DUTCH APPLE PIE

1 jar Dutch apples
or 1 (16 ounce) can of
apple pie filling

1 unbaked pie crust

Pie crust can be homemade or store bought. Place apples in unbaked pie crust.

Crust topping:

½ cup sugar
¾ cup flour

1 cut-up stick of butter

Cover with crust topping mixture made by mixing sugar and flour and cutting in the softened butter with pastry cutter or 2 table knives. Should resemble a crumbled texture. Completely cover the apples with the crust topping mixture. Bake at 400 degrees for 45 minutes. Remove from oven and cool on cake rack.

Serves 8

Carol Ann Roberts Dumond

GRANDMA'S FAMOUS PUMPKIN PIE

1 large can pumpkin
1½ cups sugar
2 teaspoons cinnamon
½ whole grated nutmeg
(more if small)
6 eggs, slightly beaten

1 (13 ounce) can
evaporated milk
2¼ cups milk
1 (8 inch) pie crust
and 2 (9 inch) pie crusts

Preheat oven to 450 degrees. Stir all ingredients. Pour into pastries and bake for 10 minutes at 450 degrees. Then continue baking at 325 degrees for 45 minutes or until knife comes out clean.

(2) 9 inch pies and (1) 8 inch pie

Kathleen V. Rudick

Lemon Cheese Cake Pie

Crust:

1 box vanilla wafers   ½ cup butter

Melt the butter and crush the vanilla wafers. Mix together to make the crumb crust. Press into 9 inch pie pan.

Filling:

1 (8-ounce) package cream
   cheese
2 tablespoons butter
½ cup sugar
1 egg
2 tablespoons flour

⅔ cup milk
¼ cup fresh lemon juice
1 tablespoon grated lemon
   peel
1 teaspoon vanilla

Cream cheese and butter, add sugar and egg. Mix well. Mix in flour, milk, and stir in lemon juice and peel. Pour into unbaked vanilla wafer shell. Bake 35 minutes at 350 degrees.

Topping:

½ pint sour cream   1 teaspoon vanilla
2 tablespoons sugar

Mix sour cream, sugar and vanilla together. Raise the oven to 425 degrees and spread topping over pie. Bake for 5 minutes. Chill before serving.

12 servings

Marianne Schneider

Lemon Ice Box Pie

1 can sweetened condensed
   milk
¼ cup fresh lemon juice
½ pint (8 ounces) frozen
   whipped topping

1 small can crushed
   pineapple, drained
2 cups finely chopped
   pecans
1 (9-inch) graham cracker
   crust

Mix condensed milk with fresh lemon juice. Add well drained pineapple and nuts. Fold in whipped topping. Pour into crust and chill at least 3 hours. Garnish with lemon slices.

Lise Anne Dumond Slatten

"Puh-Kahn"

They say Crayfish, we say Crawfish. They say Pee-Kan, we say Puh-Kahn. And our Northern friends are as fascinated by our Pecan Pies as they are by our crawfish dishes. Regardless of how you say it, pecan pie is a true Southern treat.

Our house had an abundance of pecan trees, and on an Autumn afternoon it was easy to gather buckets full. Searching for the nuts, as they nestled under newly-fallen leaves and broad, thick blades of St. Augustine grass, was akin to the fun of an Easter Egg Hunt.

A basket of pecans always rested on the kitchen counter, with a nutcracker and pick nearby. Anyone industrious enough to produce a cup and a half of shelled pecans quite understandably expected a pecan pie as a reward.

I cannot imagine a Thanksgiving or Christmas meal without pecan pie.

Southern Pecan Pie

Prepared pie shell

Mix:

   1 cup granulated sugar
   1 cup white Karo syrup
   2 tablespoons melted butter
   ¼ teaspoon salt
   3 beaten eggs
   1 ½ cups pecan halves

Pour into pie shell. Bake at 400 degrees for 15 minutes. Reduce to 350 degrees and bake for another 30 minutes. Remove from oven and let cool on cake rack.

Carol Ann Roberts Dumond

RITZ CRACKER PIE

25 crushed Ritz crackers	1 tablespoon vanilla
1 cup finely chopped pecans	½ tablespoon baking powder
¾ cup sugar	1 carton Cool Whip
3 egg whites	3 ounces cream cheese

Whip egg whites until stiff and gradually add other ingredients, except for whipped cream and cream cheese. Bake in pie plate at 300 degrees for 30 minutes. Let cool. Mix cream cheese and cool whip and spread over pie.

Serves 8.

Janie Smith

BAKED CUSTARD

8 eggs	7 cups milk (use part half &
1 ½ cups sugar	half if desired for richer
1 tablespoon vanilla	custard)

Separate eggs and beat the egg yolks. Add sugar, vanilla and milk. Beat the egg whites until stiff and fold into the egg and milk mixture. Mix well. Spoon with ladle into custard cups and set cups in hot water in pans. Bake in preheated 400 degree oven until brown. Reduce oven temperature to 300 degrees until set - about 1 hour. Test with small knife to see if knife comes out clean.

Marianne Schneider

SHELLING, SHUCKING & SNAPPING

While I didn't grow up on a farm, I will always be grateful that my parents introduced us to many of the activities that make farm life special. They saw to it that we learned that fresh fruits and vegetables didn't just appear on the table through some magical manufacturing process at the grocery store. They let us (sometimes made us) experience things like harvesting, shelling, shucking and snapping. At times, it just seemed like plain old hard work, but looking back, it gave us an appreciation for the process through which America is fed and some precious memories of family togetherness.

Among my memories are gathering and preparing peaches, blackberries, pecans, snap beans, field peas and corn. Our efforts always earned a wonderful reward, as Mom prepared a delicious dish with the fruits of our labor. I remember one particular hot day when we were lead into a field to break corn. It was a gruesome task for a young child, but afterward, Mom made corn soup from the fresh, tender ears, and somehow it tasted even better because we had picked it ourselves.

Picking blackberries which grew wild around our property was not as grueling, but the reward was equally wonderful as we ate them sprinkled with sugar or waited with eager anticipation for them to be turned into a

BLACKBERRY COBBLER

Crust Layer:
    1 cup evaporated milk
    1 cup flour
    3 teaspoons baking powder
    1 cup sugar
    1 teaspoon vanilla
       Pinch of salt

Mix crust layer ingredients together well. Pour into 9 x 12 inch greased pan.

Blackberry Layer:
    1 tablespoon cornstarch
    ½ cup boiling water
    ¾ cup sugar
    3 cups blackberries (fresh or
       frozen)
       Butter
       Cinnamon

Mix together blackberry layer ingredients. Pour slowly into middle of cobbler batter, dot with butter and sprinkle with cinnamon. Bake in 350 degree oven for 45 minutes.

The fruit goes to the bottom with a golden cobbler on top.

Serves 8

Mrs. Bruno Kidder

blackberry cobbler or dumplings. There was a similar incentive for picking and shelling pecans; we knew that they would end up in Dad's delicious pralines or Mom's wonderful pies or cookies.

Memories of food seem more special when you have picked the ingredients yourself from nature's bounty and seen them go from the fields and meadows to the warmth of our family kitchen.

Fruit Pizza

1 roll refrigerator sugar
cookie dough
1 (8 ounce) package cream
cheese, softened

½ cup sugar
½ teaspoon vanilla

Suggested fruits:
Strawberries, blueberries,
kiwi, peaches, bananas or
any soft fruit, sliced

Glaze:
1 cup apricot preserves

1 tablespoon water

Spray pizza pan with Pam. Roll out dough dusting with flour. Place in pan, making a small ridge around edge of pan. Bake according to directions on package. Cool. Cream together cream cheese, sugar and vanilla. Mix until smooth and spread over cooked cookie. Arrange fruit on top of mixture in any pattern you wish. Brush glaze over fruit and cream cheese mixture. Cut with pizza cutter and serve.

Acadiana Culinary Classic 1992 Le Petit Classique first place winner.

Molly Reid

BRAZILIAN CHOCOLATE MOUSSE

¾ cup sugar
1 envelope unflavored
   gelatin
6 eggs, separated
2½ cups milk

2 squares (2 ounces)
   unsweetened grated
   chocolate
1 cup ground cocktail
   peanuts
½ teaspoon vanilla

In a saucepan, thoroughly stir together sugar and gelatin. In a bowl beat egg yolks slightly; add milk and beat to combine; stir into gelatin mixture. Add chocolate. Cook over medium-high heat, stirring constantly, just until mixture comes to a boil. Cool thoroughly at room temperature. Stir in ground peanuts and vanilla. Beat egg whites until stiff; fold into chocolate mixture. Pour into serving dishes and chill until firm. Garnish with sweetened whipped cream and chopped peanuts.

12 to 14 servings

Mary Usner

MAW-MAW'S BREAD PUDDING

Bread Pudding:

8 slices stale bread (or raisin
   bread)
6 eggs
1 cup milk plus 2
   tablespoons

5 tablespoons sugar
3 tablespoons melted butter
   or oleo
1 teaspoon vanilla extract

Mix all ingredients well and place in dish and then place the dish in a pan of water. Bake in 350 degree oven for 1 hour or until knife inserted comes out clean.

Sauce:

3 egg whites
4 tablespoons sugar

1 teaspoon vanilla

Beat until stiff. Cover pudding with sauce. Place in 350 degree oven until brown.

12 servings

Elizabeth Bourque Preis

HOME REMEDY

Miss Lou, a beloved school teacher in Breaux Bridge, Louisiana, did not consider herself a cook. Her expertise, she claimed emphatically, was in teaching and in playing the organ at church. But her arguments to the contrary, Miss Lou's bread pudding would have commanded a place of honor at the most lavish epicurean feast.

Now, Miss Lou's bread pudding was not a dish prepared for consumption at the normal dining hour. It was something she fixed for those who were ill. Being sick is never fun, but the burden was lightened immeasurably when Miss Lou's Bread Pudding was prescribed for the patient. For its full healing powers, "Miss Lou's Bread Pudding to Make You Well" had to be served from an antique tureen from France. I strongly recommend that procedure today, if you want the full delight of this special dish.

BREAD PUDDING

6 well beaten eggs
1 stick melted butter
2 cups half & half cream
2 cups milk
¾ cup sugar
4 hamburger buns

Topping:
1 tablespoon cinnamon
⅓ cup sugar

Combine eggs, butter, half & half, milk and sugar. Add hamburger buns. Place in a greased 9 x 12 inch pan. Sprinkle with mixture of topping ingredients. Bake at 350 degrees for 45 to 50 minutes.

8 to 10 servings

Tammy Phillips

Bayou Benoit is a tiny community deep in Louisiana's great Atchafalaya Swamp. What a wonderful experience it was spending weekends at our family camp there when I was a child.

The surroundings were primitive, but the kitchen of our camp was a warm and wonderful place where my grandmother presided—and taught us the basics of true Cajun cooking. Ma Ma taught us to make bouillabaisse, etouffee, gumbo, oreilles de cochon, and much more. She was the best cook I had ever known, and she passed along to us the authentic Cajun culinary traditions, there in the awesome surroundings of the world's largest river bottom swamp.

Ironically, my favorite among all the foods she taught us to cook does not have a Cajun name. It is Caramel Cup Custard, and while it may not sound Cajun, it has topped off some of the best Cajun meals—and calls up some of the best Cajun memories—of my life.

CARAMEL CUP CUSTARD

1 cup sugar
2 cups half & half
3 cups milk
4 eggs & 8 egg yolks
1 cup powdered sugar
2 teaspoons vanilla

Caramel: Melt 1 cup sugar in a heavy pot. Cook sugar until it is a golden color - pour into custard cups. Custard: Bring cream and milk to a boil. Beat eggs, yolks and sugar until thick, slowly add hot milk to egg mixture. Mix well - Pour into cups - Bake at 325 degrees in a water bath for 1 hour.

Cheryl Guilbeau

DELIGHTFUL LAYERED DESSERT

Crust:
- ½ cup butter
- ½ cup finely chopped pecans
- 1 cup flour
- 2 tablespoons powdered sugar

Melt butter, mix with flour, nuts, and sugar. Pat firmly onto bottom of 8 x 11 inch glass baking dish. Bake for 20 minutes in 350 degree oven. Cool well.

Filling Layer One:
- 8 ounces cream cheese
- 1 cup Cool Whip
- 1 cup powdered sugar

Mix softened cream cheese and powdered sugar. Add Cool Whip and mix well. Spread over cooled crust.

Filling Layer Two:
- 1 large box chocolate instant pudding mix
- 2⅔ cups of milk

Mix following pie directions on pudding box. Spread over layer one.

Topping:
- Remainder of Cool Whip
- 1 or more of the following - chocolate bar, Heath bar chips, chopped nuts

Spread with Cool Whip making swirls. Sprinkle with chocolate curls (with vegetable peeler shave along edge of chocolate bar), Heath bar chips, and/or chopped nuts. Refrigerate for at least 6 hours.

Connie Galloway

Éclair Dessert

⅓ cup cocoa
1 cup sugar
¼ cup milk
1 stick of butter
1 teaspoon vanilla

1 large package instant
  vanilla pudding
3 cups milk
1 (8-ounce) carton frozen
  whipped cream
Graham crackers

Stir together cocoa, sugar and milk in saucepan. Boil 1 minute, stirring well. Remove from heat and add butter and vanilla. Stir until butter is melted. Set aside. Make pudding as directed on box. Fold in Cool Whip. Line bottom of 9 x 12 inch Pyrex pan with graham crackers. Top with ½ of the pudding mixture, then layer again, ending with the graham crackers. Pour cooled chocolate sauce over top and refrigerate at least 1 day for the best flavor.

Bonnie Broussard
Debbie Foreman

Lemon Sherbet

1 (6-ounce) can frozen
  lemonade concentrate
3 cups milk

½ cup plus 1 tablespoon
  sugar
12 drops yellow food
  coloring

Mix together and freeze in a churn-type ice cream freezer. This recipe can easily be doubled.

1 quart

Beth Landry

One of my favorite food memories is of the aroma of ginger and cinnamon on a crisp Friday evening in the Fall of the year. Before every high school football game, Mom would take my sister and me to visit my grandparents. When we walked in the door, we were greeted by that aroma and knew that "Maw-Maw" was fixing her delicious gingerbread. It was impossible for a child to be patient with that heavenly aroma in her nostrils. When the gingerbread was finally removed from the oven, my sister and I would stand by the pan for what seemed like hours, waiting for Maw-Maw to say it was cool enough to cut. Sometimes Paw-Paw would be as anxious as we were, and considerably braver. Without waiting for approval, he would cut us all a hunk of the wonderful dessert, and then—like us—beat a hasty retreat from Maw-Maw's kitchen.

MAW-MAW'S GINGERBREAD

2½ cups flour
2 tablespoons ginger
2 tablespoons cinnamon
2 teaspoons soda
2 eggs
⅔ cup shortening
1 cup dark Karo syrup
1 cup sugar
1 stick margarine
1 cup boiling water

Blend the dry ingredients. Add the remaining ingredients (boiling water last). Mix well. The batter will be thin. Pour mixture into 9 x 13 inch metal pan that has been sprayed with non-sticking cooking spray. Bake at 350 degrees for 35 minutes. Cut gingerbread into squares.

24 2-inch squares

Maw-Maw warned to "be careful not to get burned" when adding the boiling water.

Denise O. Daigre

Mamaw Lucy's Peach Cobbler

Pastry:

1 cup flour	6 tablespoons shortening
½ teaspoon salt	4 tablespoons milk

Blend flour, salt and shortening with a pastry blender. Add milk and mix well. Chill before rolling.

Filling:

6 large Ruston peaches	¾ teaspoon fresh grated
1½ cups sugar	nutmeg
2 tablespoons cornstarch	¼ teaspoon cinnamon
1½ sticks butter	

Slice peaches and combine with 1 cup sugar. Cook in saucepan until tender. Add ½ cup sugar, cornstarch, 1 stick butter, nutmeg and cinnamon. Put in 10 inch square pan. Cut pastry into strips and form a lattice top over peaches. Pour ½ stick melted butter over top. Bake in 350 degree oven for 35 to 45 minutes.

6 servings

Donna James

Mexican Apple Crêpes

2 cans cinnamon and spice apple pie filling	8 large flour tortillas

Grease a 9 x 13 inch pan with margarine. Put ¼ can pie filling on end of each tortilla and roll up. Place edge side down in pan. 8 crêpes will fit tightly in pan.

Sauce:

2 cups water	1 tablespoon vanilla
1½ cups sugar	flavoring
2 sticks margarine or butter	1 teaspoon nutmeg
1 teaspoon cinnamon	

Combine sauce ingredients and pour on top of crêpes. Bake 45 minutes at 375 degrees. While baking baste top of crêpes with sauce so top and edges do not get crusty. May be served warm with ice cream on top.

Serves 8

Teri Broussard
Iris Wiederhold

STELLA'S TREATS

Stella was our baby-sitter, and she was special. She came every Saturday, in the white uniform that she wore so proudly as a nurse's aide at a clinic for crippled children. She always liked to come early, "to cook dinner for my children." We knew that there would be peppermint sticks in the pockets of the uniform, and that there would be a delicious meal of fried chicken, rice and gravy and Popeye spinach, topped off with chocolate or vanilla ice cream from one of the two three-gallon drums that were always in our freezer.

But those were not the only treats—nor the most important. Stella brought a paper bag each Saturday, and we waited impatiently until finally it would yield its wonderful contents—Stella's delicious popcorn balls.

POPCORN BALLS

1 cup sugar
⅓ cup white corn syrup
⅓ cup water
¼ cup butter
½ teaspoon vinegar
1 teaspoon vanilla
3 quarts popped popcorn (2 large microwave bags)

Combine sugar, syrup, water, butter, salt and vinegar. Cook, stirring until sugar is dissolved. Continue cooking, without stirring until syrup reaches 270 on a candy thermometer or forms a firm ball when a little bit is dropped in a cup of cold water. Add vanilla. Pour syrup over popped popcorn, stirring until all kernels are covered. Rub butter on hands and shape into balls, about the size of a tennis ball. Make in small batches and do not double this recipe. May add color for holidays.

Carol Ann Roberts Dumond

CHOCOLATE SAUCE

My mother always believed that Reese's Peanut Butter Cups hit the market well after my family had the idea of combining chocolate and peanut butter. It was just one of the delights that developed from creative use of my grandmother's delicious chocolate sauce.

"Maw Maw" made her wonderful sauce for over 50 years. In the Thirties and Forties, she would make "chocolate sandwiches" for my mother's school lunch. Mom was very popular around lunch time, and many classmates wanted to trade their less creative sandwiches for hers.

My memories go back to childhood visits to Maw Maw's house on a sugar cane farm in the country, where we would watch her stir the chocolate sauce while she carried on a conversation with my mother and my aunts. When it was done, she would bring the hot pan to the table and start serving immediately. Her grandchildren had different ideas about the best way to enjoy the delicious sauce: on ice cream as a chocolate sundae, on plain bread as a chocolate sandwich, and with peanut butter as a fore-runner to the aforementioned peanut butter cups.

Maw Maw always made chocolate sauce for me when I visited her during my college days, and there was always some left over to be carried back to the dorm.

Maw Maw is no longer with us, but my children still remember her— and her sauce is now in its third generation as a special treat and family tradition.

SWEET NOODLE PUDDING

I have many childhood memories of meal time and the delicious dishes my mother served, but probably the one we anticipated most was her wonderful Sweet Noodle Pudding. It was a holiday treat, and I grew up asking why she only prepared it for special occasions. I make it now, and my children ask the same thing. I guess the answer is that it is a special treat, and adds something extra to a special occasion. And for me, it brings back special memories.

MEASUREMENTS AND EQUIVALENTS

Dash = less than ⅛ teaspoon
Trace = Less than ⅛ fl. teaspoon
3 teaspoons = 1 tablespoon
2 tablespoons = 1 liquid ounce = ⅛ cup
4 tablespoons = 2 liquid ounces = ¼ cup
5 tablespoons plus 1 teaspoon = ⅓ cup
8 tablespoons = 4 liquid ounces = ½ cup
16 tablespoons = 8 liquid ounces = 1 cup
2 cups = 16 liquid ounces = 1 pint
2 pints = 32 liquid ounces = 1 quart
2 quarts = 64 liquid ounces = ½ gallon
4 quarts = 128 liquid ounces = 1 gallon
Beans—16 ounces dry = cooked 6 to 7 cups
Butter or margarine—¼ pound stick = ¼ cup
Cheese—hard—4 ounces, shredded = 1 cup;
    cottage—8 ounces = 1 cup; cream—8 ounces = 1 cup
Chocolate—1 ounce = 1 square; morsels—6 ounces = 1 cup
Coconut—3 ounces, shredded – 1 cup
Coffee—1 pound = 4 cups
Cranberries—12 ounces, fresh = 3 cups
Cream—1 cup unwhipped = 2 cups whipped; sour—8 ounces = 1 cup
Crumbs (fine, dry)—3 slices bread = 1 cup; 28 saltines = 1 cup
22 vanilla wafers = 1 cup; 14-15 graham crackers = 1 cup
Dates or candied fruit—8 ounces, chopped = 1 cup
Egg—whites—8 to 10 = 1 cup; yolks—12 to 14 = 1 cup
Flour—sifted—1 pound = 4 cups; unsifted—1 pound = 3½ cups;
    cake—1 pound = 4½ cups
Garlic—1 clove = ⅛ teaspoon powdered
Gelatin, unflavored—1 envelope = 1 tablespoon
Herbs—1 tablespoon fresh = 1 teaspoon dried
Lemon juice—1 medium lemon = 3 tablespoons juice
Lime juice—1 medium lime = 2 tablespoons juice
Macaroni—1 cup = 2 cups cooked
Meat—1 pound chopped = 3 cups cooked; 1 pound ground = 2 cups cooked
Mushrooms—4 ounces canned = 8 ounces fresh
Noodles—1 cup = 1¾ cups cooked
Nuts—4 ounces, chopped = 1 cup
Onion—¼ cup fresh = 1 tablespoon dried
Orange juice—1 medium orange = ½ cup juice
Raisins—16 ounces = 2½ to 3 cups
Rice—1 pound = 2 cups; 1 cup = 3 cups cooked
Spaghetti—1 pound = 8 cups cooked
Sugar—granulated—1 pound = 2½ cups; packed brown—1 pound = 2¼ cups;
    confectioner's—1 pound = 4 to 4½ cups

SUBSTITUTIONS

Baking powder—¼ teaspoon baking soda plus ½ teaspoon cream of
    tartar = 1 teaspoon
Cornstarch—2 tablespoons flour = 1 tablespoon
Flour—½ to ⅔ tablespoon cornstarch (for thickening) = 1 tablespoon
1 cup plus 2 tablespoons sifted cake flour = 1 cup cake flour
1 cup minus 2 tablespoons sifted all-purpose flour = 1 cup flour
Milk—½ cup evaporated milk plus ½ cup water = 1 cup
Sour milk—1 cup sweet milk plus 1 tablespoon lemon juice or vinegar = 1 cup
Sugar—1⅓ cups brown sugar or 1½ cups confectioner's sugar = 1 cup

BAKING PAN SIZES

The following table will help determine substitutions of pans of similar sizes.
It's important to note that adjustments in baking times will be necessary
when pan sizes are changed.

Common Pan Size	Approximate Volume
Square and Rectangular Pans:	
8"x8"x1½" square	6 cups
8"x8"x2" square	8 cups
9"x9"x1½" square	8 cups
9"x9"x2" square	10 cups
11"x7"x2" rectangular	6 cups
13"x9"x2" rectangular	15 cups
8"x4"x2½" loaf	4 cups
8½"x4½"x2½" loaf	6 cups
9"x5"x3" loaf	8 cups
Round Pans:	
1¾"x¾" mini muffin cup	⅛ cup
2¾"x1⅛" muffin cup	¼ cup
2¾"x1⅜" muffin cup	scant ½ cup
3"x1¼" giant muffin cup	⅝ cup
8"x1¼" pie plate	3 cups
9"x1½" pie plate	4 cups
9"x2" pie plate (deep dish)	6 cups
8"x1½" cake	4 cups
8"x2" cake	7 cups
9"x1½" cake	6 cups
9"x2" cake	8½ cups
10"x2" cake	10¾ cups
9"x3" bundt	9 cups
10"x3½" bundt	12 cups
8"x3" tube	9 cups
9"x3" tube	10 cups
10"x4" tube	16 cups
9½"x2½" springform	10 cups
10"x2½" springform	12 cups

"A GATHERING OF FAMILIES"

Family gatherings and reunions were, and still are, a great source of pride for the people of South Louisiana. After God, in most cases, the family structure is the most important part of the Creole and Cajun cultures alike. Family gatherings are the backbone of this structure. On my father's side I have fifty-seven first cousins and numerous second and third cousins. I know most of them by name. The main reason for this is that we gather one day once a year in Church Point for a reunion of catching-up, introduction of newest members through birth or marriage, and renewal of friendship and love. We pray together...we eat together...we dance together...we laugh, love and share each other.

As a kid many years ago we gathered often at my grand-father's house and shared many hours of cousin-enjoyment and cousin-loving.

Floyd Sonnier

INDEX

TELL ME MORE

The Junior League of Lafayette
100 Felecie Drive
Lafayette, Louisiana 70506
(318) 988-2739 or 800-757-3651

Please send me information on ordering additional copies of *Tell Me More* and our other cookbooks, *Talk About Good!* and *Talk About Good II.*

Name: _____

Address: _____

City: _____ State: _____ Zip: _____

Phone: (   ) _____

- -

TELL ME MORE

The Junior League of Lafayette
100 Felecie Drive
Lafayette, Louisiana 70506
(318) 988-2739 or 800-757-3651

Please send me information on ordering additional copies of *Tell Me More* and our other cookbooks, *Talk About Good!* and *Talk About Good II.*

Name: _____

Address: _____

City: _____ State: _____ Zip: _____

Phone: (   ) _____

- -

TELL ME MORE

The Junior League of Lafayette
100 Felecie Drive
Lafayette, Louisiana 70506
(318) 988-2739 or 800-757-3651

Please send me information on ordering additional copies of *Tell Me More* and our other cookbooks, *Talk About Good!* and *Talk About Good II.*

Name: _____

Address: _____

City: _____ State: _____ Zip: _____

Phone: (   ) _____